THEY HAD TO GO OUT

Any referance in this book as to the
Astoria Maritime Museum should be
read as (The Columbia River Maritime
Museum), Astoria, Oregon.

The Author, Gary J. Hudson

THEY HAD TO GO OUT

The Triumph-Mermaid Tragedy

Gary J. Hudson

Cover art by Joyce C. LaCoursiere-Hudson

Library of Congress Control Number: 2008909764
ISBN: Hardcover   978-1-4363-8133-8
               Softcover   978-1-4363-8132-1

To order additional copies of this book, contact:
Xlibris Corporation
1-888-795-4274
www.Xlibris.com
Orders@Xlibris.com
52874

CONTENTS

They say you do not miss what you never had—that is not true.
I miss my dad more each day.

Cheryl Culp Blackburn
Daughter of BM1 John L. Culp

To all the Coast Guard men and women of the past and present at lifeboat
stations throughout the United States. They risk their lives on a daily basis
in the pursuit of saving life and property at sea. Some have lost.

ACKNOWLEDGMENTS

Below is a list of those who recognized and assisted the author in the collection of data and other material for this book.

Joan Miller, wife of BM1 Miller, for her editing expertise and firsthand knowledge of 12 January 1961 and of her all around support to the author in the writing of this book.

The John Culp family, his wife LaVerne, son, John Culp Jr., and daughter, Cheryl Culp Blackburn.

Colleen Simonsen, a local, lifelong resident of Hammond, Oregon.

Mrytle Kary, wife of Bud Kary and a lifelong resident of Ilwaco, Washington.

Terry Lowe, engineer onboard the *CG-40564* on 12 January 1961.

John Webb, coxswain of the *CG-36554*.

Doyle S. Porter, officer in charge, Cape Disappointment, 1961.

Warren C. Berto, officer in charge, Point Adams, 1961.

Don Davis, electronics technician, Cape Disappointment, 1961.

Dave Trujillo, lookout watch, Cape Disappointment, 12 January 1961.

Junior Meyer, engineer, North Head Light Station.

Gordon Huggins, engineer and only survivor of the MLB *Triumph*.

Jerry Glien, engineer aboard the USCGC *Yacona*, 1961.

Al Lucas, crewman aboard the *UF-1240*.

CWO Giles M. Vanderhoof, U.S. Coast Guard retired, First CO, MLBS.

Roy E. Gunnari, Coos Bay, Oregon, owner-operator of the crab boat, *Jana-Jo*.

1

They Had to Go Out

There is an addition to the above title, and that is "But You
Don't Have to Come Back."

Throughout the '30s, '40s, and '50s, the U.S. Coast Guard's thirty-six-foot motor lifeboat was the mainstay of its rescue fleet on the coasts of this country. Various versions of the boat have been around, but the last 138 of them were consistently unchanged in their construction except for the engines. As soon as diesel engines became available, they were installed in these boats. The diesel engines were much more reliable for their durability and the safety of diesel over gasoline. With the start of World War II, diesel engines were the most commonly used in boats with the General Motors diesel being the most widely used.

These boats were double-ended, heavy wood constructed with a two-ton bronze keel. The boats were built to have a positive self-righting capability. They were everything you would want in a lifeboat except for speed. All who operated them loved the boat. As long as you had water under the keel to float the boat or were operating in thirty- to forty-foot seas, the thirty-six footer would earn the reputation as a survivor. They had been rolled and pitch-poled, both stern and bow over. The boats have been washed up on the beach and came through anything that was thrown at them.

The thirty-six-foot motor lifeboats have survived when their crews did not. All of the Coast Guard boats have an assigned number; the first two numbers will designate the length of the vessel. This was the case not only for small boats, but also for vessels through ninety-five feet. On 5 February 1946, the U.S. Coast Guard's lifeboat station at Willapa Bay, twenty miles north of the Columbia River, received a telephone call stating that two crab boats were overdue at Westport, Washington. There had been a storm the previous day, and the seas and bar conditions remained very rough with twenty- to twenty-five-foot swells from the southwest. Conditions were enhanced by winds of twenty to thirty knots from the same direction. Coast Guard station Grays Harbor, fifteen miles north of Willapa Bay, had sent the fifty-two-foot motor lifeboat *Invincible* out to search and had requested that Willapa send out the *CG-36384*.

The four-man crew consisted of Chief Boatswain Joe Miller, Machinist Mate First Class Geloyd Simmons, Coxswain Jim R. Graves, and Seaman First Class Howard Hampton. In those days, the only clothing the crews had for protection from the elements was foul-weather coats, rain pants, jackets, and hats. There were plenty of the heavy kapok life jackets, but at times, they were not worn. They were difficult to work in because of their bulkiness. The crews of the time did not have safety belts, as they do today, but as a measure of protection, they would tie themselves to the boat with a short piece of line that would still enable them limited movement about the boat.

It was approximately 1:00 AM on 5 February when the thirty-six footer made a brief rendezvous with the *Invincible* north of Willapa Bay. Both boats went their separate ways searching for any evidence of a boat or persons in distress. Later on that day, the *CG-36384* was found washed up on the beach ten miles north of Grays Harbor near Ocean City with no one aboard. Three of the lost crew members were recovered on the beach north of Grays Harbor; the body of the fourth man would never be found. Records do not say if the men found were wearing life jackets. If they had been strapped securely to the boat, perhaps they would have survived. These boats were the toughest of their era.

It was later discovered that the two missing crab boats had been safely anchored inside Willapa Bay even before the Coast Guard boats were dispatched to look for them. The most logical thought is that it was very dark out, and the crew was running just outside of the surf line and was caught broadside by a sneaker wave. While the crew was running in what they thought might be safer waters, they were hit by this much larger wave that had been generated from far offshore. The boat most likely rolled, ejecting all hands.

Another incident involving a thirty-six-foot motor lifeboat needs to be mentioned as it attests to the ruggedness and survivability of the boats. This boat was the *CG-36554* based out of lifeboat station Cape Disappointment, Ilwaco, Washington. The incident happened on 11 February 1965.

At approximately 9:00 PM, a West Coast Airlines plane was en route from Aberdeen, Washington, to Astoria, Oregon. The pilot had been flying parallel and offshore from the Long Beach Peninsula, a twenty-eight-mile sandy shoreline north of the Columbia River in Washington State. Out of a side window, the pilot observed what appeared to be a light flashing an SOS signal. The exact location, he assumed, was just off the beach approach road from Long Beach, Washington. He called the airport in Astoria and relayed the information to them. They, in turn, had placed a call to the new Coast Guard air station at Tongue Point located on a point of land jutting out into the Columbia River just outside the city of Astoria, Oregon. Three helicopters were attached to this station. A call was also placed to the Coast Guard station Cape Disappointment because of its locality to the area of the sighting. The air station would shortly send a HH-52A amphibious helicopter to search the area.

At Cape Disappointment, Chief Paul Miller (no relation to the Miller in the aforementioned *CG-36384* incident) who had, just the week before, been promoted to chief readied a boat and beach patrol crew. Miller was to depart as coxswain of the *CG-36554* with Engineman First Class Dick Joffe and, Boatswains Mate Second Class Larry Edwards would take the station's jeep that was equipped with a radio to the beach area.

Edwards dropped the boat crew off at the boathouse and departed for the area off Long Beach. Very shortly, after Edwards dropped them off, Miller and his crew were underway in the thirty-six footer. Even with the darkness Miller had little difficulty crossing a favorable bar. He rounded Peacock Spit well offshore to not accidently get caught by an unexpected breaking sea and headed north outside the beach surf line. There were approximately ten- to twelve-foot-long rolling swells heading to the beach from the west. Miller tried to stay far enough offshore so as not to get inside the surf line.

Even though the sandy beach area was very straight, heading in a northerly direction, it was a different story concerning the bottom contours offshore. Strong currents to the north could change the bottom contours almost daily. At times, bottom sands would be consistent for long stretches, and then the currents would move the sand around, piling it underwater to form small spits that would jut seaward from shore.

These spits could be recognized from both ashore and at sea during daylight hours. This was accomplished by observing a line of breakers running parallel to the beach, but in an effected area, the breakers would start much farther out, indicating sandbars. In the darkness, it could be a much different situation. While running parallel and outside the surf line and before realizing it, the coxswain would come across an underwater shoal, and the breakers in this area would start outside of his location. All of a sudden, he would find himself in the middle of breaking surf. Chief Miller's idea was to travel north and not enter any surf unless they saw something inshore signifying a distress situation.

BM2 Larry Edwards arrived at the beach approach road about the same time the helicopter got there to begin the search. Edwards located the Long Beach chief of police, John Winnick, and another resident who stated that when they arrived on the beach, they had spotted a light offshore. They said that it appeared to be moving in a northerly direction and away from them. Nevertheless, a search had to be conducted, and Edwards relayed the information to the helicopter and *CG-36554*.

Chief Miller arrived in the area offshore from Long Beach at 10:00 PM. He could see the lights on the beach, and he observed the helicopter flying back and forth searching. Occasionally the helicopter would fly over the lifeboat. What happened next came very quick. Miller looked to his left and saw white water outside of his position. He brought the boat to full power and turned it hard to port, bringing the bow around and into the seas. He knew well what was coming at him, and he wanted to get into a position that would be more favorable to him and his engineers' survival. The bow started to rise sharply, and the wave broke right over the top of the boat. The boat did not come through the breaker, but pitch-poled bow over onto its top.

On the beach, Edwards had been observing the helicopter and boat search offshore. While looking at the boat lights, he noticed something very odd. He saw a set of running lights heading straight toward the beach, but they were reversed with the red to the left and the green to the right. No sooner had he noticed this, then all the lights on the lifeboat went out. He immediately called the helicopter and told them that he thought something had happened to the *CG-36554* and asked them to investigate.

Aboard the *CG-36554*, Chief Miller had a death grip on the wheel and knew that the boat had just righted after capsizing. It was very quiet with no engine running and the lights out. Normally when a boat capsizes, the engine remains running; but as Miller pressed the starter button to restart, nothing happened. At the same time, he noticed that his engineer was missing. He then heard him yelling for help from the water. The engineer was able to swim to the side of the boat, and Miller reached over and pulled him aboard.

When the breaker had capsized the boat, it had carried it some distance toward shore. Soon they could feel and hear the boat bouncing off the bottom. The helicopter quickly arrived over the boat and hoisted both men aboard. Paul had some bumps and bruises, but the engineer was suffering from shock, exposure, and a possible back injury. The helicopter dropped Miller off on the dry beach by Edwards and then proceeded to the hospital in Astoria with the engineer.

Shortly after the crew was removed from the *CG-36554*, the boat drifted far enough up on the beach so that Edwards could get a line on it to the jeep. The boat was held in position the rest of the night. The helicopter returned at daylight to better search the area but came up with negative results for anyone in distress.

Also at daylight, a truck with a lowboy trailer and a large crawler tractor from a nearby jetty project were brought to the beach to salvage the boat. It only took a few hours to load the boat and remove it from the beach to a main roadway. The boat was trucked to the Coast Guard base at Tongue Point, Astoria, Oregon, where it would be checked from stem to stern. There it was found that the batteries had shifted, and a cable had come loose. This was the reason Miller could not restart the engine.

Other than the battery cable problem and a few broken, cracked ribs that were replaced with new ribs that would be placed next to the defective ribs and secured with screws from the outside, there was very little damage. The boat was returned to service shortly after repairs were made. If the batteries had remained connected, most probably, Miller could have restarted the engine and continued on the mission.

Steps were taken after this incident to ensure that the batteries were secured properly in all thirty-six-foot motor lifeboats in the Coast Guard. One thing that Chief Miller did lose was his brand new chief's hat that he had only worn for one week. In spite of losing his hat, he did feel very grateful that no lives were lost.

While on the beach that night, BM2 Edwards did notice some young men with flashlights walking on the beach. It was discussed among the beach party that possibly one of these men had sent the signal. Police Chief Winnick said he would follow up on it.

A couple of days after the incident, a young man from Long Beach confessed to being the person that signaled a false distress. The following is from his letter to the Coast Guard station Cape Disappointment.

Dear Mr. Miller & Mr. Joffee.

This letter is to apologize for my thoughtlessness on the beach Wednesday night. I had no idea there would be any repercussions or I would have never flashed that light. I promise I will never do it again. Please accept my apology.

The U.S. Coast Guard's motto is Semper Paratus, meaning Always Ready. The Coast Guard has participated in every conflict that this country has been in from 1790 through today. Along with defending their country, the men have lived up to the motto Always Ready. They risked (and sometimes lost their lives) during hundreds of recues and attempted rescues of their fellow seaman in distress. They did so from pulling boats in the beginning with equipment and manpower against the seas to using power lifeboats today. The old boats were all very antiquated by today's standards.

CG-36554 on beach 1963, BMC Paul Miller in foreground.

2

Fifty-two-foot Motor Lifeboat

The U.S. Coast Guard Lifeboat Station Grays Harbor at Westport, Washington, is located approximately forty five miles north of the mouth of the Columbia River. The bar is the entrance for shipping to the ports of Aberdeen and Hoquiam. There is also a large recreational and commercial fleet of fishing boats at Westport.

In 1959, the U.S. Coast Guard motor lifeboat station at Westport was the home of the fifty-two-foot wooden motor lifeboat *Invincible*. She was one of only two of this type built in 1935. Her sister boat, the *Triumph*, was stationed at lifeboat station Point Adams on the Columbia River at Hammond, Oregon. At Westport, the U.S. Coast Guard also had two forty-foot utility boats, one thirty-foot utility boat, and two of the very dependable thirty-six-foot MLBs (motor lifeboat).

The *Invincible* was identical to the *Triumph* in all her good points and her flaws of which there were many. The first and foremost flaw was that both boats had exhaust stacks that could allow water to enter the engine under certain conditions, which could cause engine failure. It is not understood why this was a feature of these two boats. At the time of their construction, shipbuilders were building the motorized thirty-six footers with the T exhaust out each side of the hull, which would allow water to enter on one side and exit on the other without causing the engine, due to backpressure, to be disabled. Contrary to many beliefs, these two boats were not built to be self-righting like the thirty-six footers, but their stability was said to be very high with an engineered positive righting capability from around 137 degrees. In fact, if turned over, this boat would more than likely float upside down unless righted by sea action.

A second flaw was that the superstructures were made of bronze, which added around 1,700 pounds above the main deck. The weight of the superstructure was figured into the 137-degree righting factor, but if the superstructure would have been made of wood, the degree of roll that could have been recovered could have been increased. For some reason, since the construction of these two boats, the engineered statistics as to the righting capabilities were always ignored. The boats were always considered fully self-righting from a 180-degree capsizing.

Flaw 3 was that the tow bit was not located forward of the screw so that the boat, while towing on an entrance bar, could maneuver ninety degrees to its tow if needed. In other words, if the boat had to make a sharp turn, it could pivot at the tow bit. With the tow bit aft and over the screw, towing a boat in that manner could put the towing boat in what is called irons (locked into a position where it is unable to maneuver). Flaw 4, the aft lifelines had to be lowered before towing, leaving crew members working aft vulnerable to being washed overboard. Flaw 5 was that the coxswain's vision of the tow bit and the crew working the lines aft was blocked by a five-foot high structure called a doghouse that was the entrance into an aft berthing area. Another item to mention is that there was only one way in and one way out of the compartments. These flaws were very apparent to the educated seaman and were not the characteristics you would want in a lifeboat.

In the winter of 1959-60, the crew at Grays Harbor took the *Invincible* out to escort a crab boat back in across the entrance bar that happened to be very rough at the time. It is not understood whether the crab boat asked for this assistance or that the crew of the *Invincible* used this as an excuse to go on some breaker drills.

On the way out and still on the inside of the Grays Harbor bar, the *Invincible* passed the crab boat, which had already crossed the bar to safety. Venturing out further into the bar area, they encountered large breaking seas. They decided to turn around and head back inside the bar. It was during this turn that a breaker hit them broad side and nearly capsized them. The *Invincible* came back upright with all the crew onboard, but the water had disabled the engine by entering the exhaust stack. The *Invincible* put out a call for help, and this was overheard by the crab boat, which was safely inside the bar. The crabber had two men onboard and immediately, as was the tradition of the sea, turned the boat around and headed out to help the *Invincible*. When they arrived on scene, the *Invincible* had managed to start the engine and was heading into safety inside the bar. The crew of the crab boat made the turn to head back in and took a large breaker, tearing the cabin and crew right off the boat. Both fishermen were killed.

The foregoing is written as testament to what happened because of one of the major flaws in the construction of the two wooden fifty-two footers in 1935-36.

These two boats had operated until 1959, being involved in the saving of numerous lives and property. They were great boats for driving through heavy seas as long as you did this "bow on." The bow of the boat is normally the strongest and offers the least resistance to large waves. If the boat was allowed to get into a broadside condition with the breakers, they could risk capsizing in which they might not recover. Modern lifeboats have a positive righting capability built into them. By modern lifeboats, I would like to state that of all of them built after 1960; none of them have been lost by capsizing to 180 degrees (of which there were many). They all recovered. However, there were a very few lost due to mechanical and human error from being put on the rocks.

Shortly after the incident with the *Invincible* at Westport, the boat was transported to a boatyard in Seattle where several modifications were made. Of these, a new T exhaust was installed, the aft doghouses to the engine room and aft berthing area were removed, and deck scuttles were installed. The deck scuttles replaced the doghouses and were made of steel with a quick-acting watertight hatch. Each scuttle protruded about one foot above the deck and, when opened, was large enough for a man to enter and climb down a ladder to the compartment below. A small steel pipe tow rail about two feet high was installed around the aft deck. This allowed the towline, when deployed, to ride on top and provided some protection for the crew from being washed overboard. After the modifications were completed, the boat was returned to serve at Westport until the new steel fifty-two footer arrived. One of the new steel fifty-two-foot MLBs, the *CG-52313*, was being built in 1959-60 at the Coast Guard Yard. The new lifeboat was due to be delivered to Station Grays Harbor at Westport in 1960. In the early fall of 1960, BM1 (boatswains mate first class) Rolland Miller went with a crew to take delivery of the new fifty-two footer. They transported her down the coast and were met outside the Grays Harbor bar by the MLB *Invincible*. This was a symbolic gesture of the old to the new in an escort across the bar. By comparison, the boats had nothing in common except that they were both fifty-two feet long and their bows and sterns came to a point. Just looking at the *CG-52313*, the boat just seemed to say, "I am the best motor lifeboat the world has seen, and I am a survivor." This viewpoint was proven to be true by this boat and her three sister boats well into the twenty-first century.

The *CG-52301* (MLB *Triumph*) at Lifeboat Station Point Adams on the Columbia River, for some reason, was not taken out of service for the upgrading of the exhaust system and other modifications that were completed on the *Invincible*.

Some other things can be said about the new fifty-two-foot steel motor lifeboats. It would seem that the Coast Guard would learn from its mistakes in the design of the older boats. However, this was not the case back then. The reasoning behind the through-hull exhaust system on the thirty-six footers and the lack of it on the old wood fifty-two footers has already been discussed. All four of the new fifty-two-foot twin-engine motor lifeboats were delivered with separate side exhausts for each engine. Taking heavy seas on one side would, at times, push water back up the exhaust, creating enough backpressure to disable the engine and even cause severe internal damage such as bending exhaust valves. It would take the Coast Guard several years to change these boats over so that both engine exhausts would converge at a T so it could exit either side of the boat. Each engine exhaust would enter a through-hull exhaust pipe. These boats, as great as they were, had another problem. There were no hydraulic assists with the steering mechanism.

The steering wheels were connected to the rudder by chain and cable. At times, it would take brute force to turn the wheel or hang on to it when backing into large seas. Letting one's grip up on the spokes of the steering wheel would cause the wheel to spin wildly from forces of the sea generated against the rudder. This action could cause serious injury to the coxswain.

After the arrival of the *CG-52313* at Westport, the old wooden *Invincible* with all of the improvements was transferred to Coos Bay, Oregon, to serve as a lifeboat at the Coast Guard station there. Around the end of November 1960 or early December 1960, Boatswains Mate First Class Floyd Shelton of the Coos Bay station brought a crew up to Westport and took delivery of the *Invincible*. On the way south, they stopped by Point Adams. Shelton stated that he had a discussion with Boatswains Mate First Class Culp of Point Adams regarding the use of the new nylon line that the *Invincible* had over the manila line that was still onboard the *Triumph*.

The manila line that the U.S. Coast Guard had been using on all of its vessels was replaced in the early sixties with three-stranded nylon line of various sizes. The nylon line was far superior to the manila line in that it had a much higher degree of strength than the manila of the same size; it would stretch up to 15 percent before parting and was resistant to mildew and rot.

On 19 December 1960, BM1 Shelton took a crew of four others out on the *Invincible* for what they called heavy-weather drills on the Coos Bay bar. All the men had life jackets on but were not tied to the boat, and soon they were in heavy rolling swells. One caught them on the bow quarter and broke over the boat, rolling her 180 degrees. Everyone, but Shelton, was ejected from the boat. The *Invincible* righted herself very quickly, and Shelton found that the rest of his crew was missing. The engine was still running, but the reduction gear seemed to be jammed in the forward position. He observed his men in the water not far away and maneuvered the boat in a circle to approach the engineer. He went up to him at the slowest speed possible and, when he thought it was right, ran over to the side and laid on the deck with his arm overboard as far as possible.

It worked out great with Shelton, saying his engineer grabbed his lower arm and just seemed to crawl right up it to the deck. As soon as the engineer was aboard, he fixed the reduction gear problem, and Shelton had full control of the boat again. They quickly maneuvered to pick up the rest of the crew.

Although no one was hurt in the above incident and the boat had performed almost flawlessly, the boat later—in 1961—was transferred to station Neah Bay, Washington. This lifeboat station was located a few miles inside the Strait of Juan de Fuca and had no bar area. The boat stayed there for a few years and then was decommissioned and later sold at public auction.

It is not understood why the *Invincible* with its new exhaust and other modifications was not taken to Point Adams and put in service in place of the *Triumph*. Then the *Triumph* could have been sent for the new installation. If this had been done, there might have been a big difference to what happened on 12 January 1961 on the Columbia River bar.

Sometime in the 1950s, there was an engine swap between the *Triumph* and the *Invincible*. The original on the *Triumph* was removed, and a General Motors 110 diesel was installed. As far as bulk and weight, the GMC was about half the size of the original engine. Don Fasterban of EMCO shipyard (no longer in existence) in Astoria, Oregon (who had done work on the original *Triumph*), said that someone, in 1961, had inquired about the engine swap. They wanted to know if any ballast had been added to the *Triumph* to compensate for the loss. He said that, as far as he remembered, this had not been done, and that he did not see any ballast on the *Triumph*.

He has also stated that he had heard from some of the locals that on a prior case to 12 January 1961, the *Triumph* had lost about half of its main towing hawser, and that it had not been replaced. This could not be further substantiated. If operating in very large seas, it would be imperative that as much line to the tow would be let out so that you would have a dip in the towline between the two boats. In other words, enough line out so that, during the tow, the dip in the line between the boats would not break water. This way, it would give a cushioning effect, act as a shock absorber, and lessen the strain on the towline. While trying to maneuver a lifeboat in the surf and towing of a boat under these conditions, it might not be possible to let out more line than would be required to get the boats to safer waters.

In 1937, the *Triumph*, soon after her arrival at Point Adams, became what was known as a gold medal boat. While on a mission back then, a crewmember was awarded the Gold Lifesaving Medal for his actions; his name was John F. McCormick.

It had been common knowledge among those that served aboard the fifty-two-foot wood lifeboats that the boats had a built-in self-righting capability. This was especially adamant from some of the old timers that served on them over the years. This seemed to be the thought of all until an investigative report of marine casualty dated 28 February 1961 from the commander of the Thirteenth Coast Guard District was found. This report clarified that neither of the fifty-two-foot wood lifeboats were guaranteed self-righting beyond 140-degree rolls. This letter will be discussed in its entirety later in this book.

MLB Triumph, CG-52301 from Pt. Adams in 1961 configuration.

MLB Invincible, CG-52300 from Westport in 1960 configuration, Note removal of aft dog houses, new taff rail and exhaust port on hull.

Plaque issued by the Coast Guard in remembrance of the lose of 2 fisherman 19 January 1960 while they were trying to assist the MLB Invincible which was disabeled on the Grays Harbor bar.

3

The Forty-foot Utility Boat

Finally, we come to that great boat—the forty-foot *utility* boat. The word *utility* says it all. During its service with the Coast Guard, it was the backbone of the boats used for all search-and-rescue calls in the ocean and inland waters.

This boat's life span with the Coast Guard ranged from the 1940s into the 1970s and was originally built of wood. In the fifties, this same boat was built in great quantities of steel with an aluminum cabin. The boats, in both configurations, were equipped with twin General Motors 671 diesel engines. Also included were twin-disc reduction gearboxes. Both were a very proven and reliable package. The boats had a planning V-hull forward and a flat bottom aft, and all could do twenty plus miles per hour. In this configuration and speed, the hull would rise out of the water and ride on the flatter portion from amidships to the stern. There was a lot of competition between engineering departments of the units where these boats were assigned to see who could tweak (fine-tune) the most RPMs and speed from their individual boat.

In the fifties and into the seventies, you could find these boats assigned to almost all lifeboat stations throughout the Coast Guard. As stated before, these boats were great when used within their limits but, being assigned to open ocean units, would lead to their use in sea conditions that, at times, were beyond their limits. The speed was nice to have, but speed alone could not always keep the boat out of trouble when crossing a hazardous bar, especially when the coxswain failed to see the danger ahead.

The forty footer originally had large windows in the forward part of the cabin, but it was quickly learned that these could not hold back breaking seas over the bow of the boat. In the early sixties, this brought about the removal of these windows, and they were replaced with what were called bar windows. All three forward windows were removed, and they were replaced with solid aluminum panels with small rectangular five-by-twelve-inch windows in the center of the panels. This addition also led to the feeling that the boat could handle larger sea conditions than what they actually were designed to experience.

The forty-footer when built, had both inside-outside steering stations, but the inside steering was removed because it was never used, and this boat was always operated from the outside. The boat had limited self-bailing capabilities in the outside deck area in four places. If the well deck were ever to fill up with water, the boat would become very sluggish and hard to control, and if one engine failed, there was not enough power to drive the boat forward to drain the deck.

This could result in a very dangerous situation and greatly increases the risk of losing the boat and crew. One problem that most steel forty-footers had was that with repeated poundings, the hull would develop cracks. Most forty-footers operating in coastal areas had, at one time or another, developed cracks that resulted in double plates being welded over the cracks. At times, sections of the hull were removed, and new plate welded in.

These boats were used in some situations along the coast in very hazardous sea conditions where getting there quickly was the top priority. Some were lost. The forty-footers were not self-righting lifeboats even though their coxswains at times put them into these situations. On 12 January 1961, the decision was made to take the *CG-40564* from Life Boat Station Cape Disappointment on a call across the Columbia River bar to assist a crab boat that was in immediate danger.

The *CG-40564* would go into conditions that were almost beyond her ability to cope with during that particular rescue attempt. Through the crew's valiant efforts, they managed to tow the boat to the vicinity of buoy 1. After being relieved of the tow by the MLB *Triumph*, the almost fateful decision was made to try to return to safe haven across the bar. This decision would most certainly have put the boat beyond the crew's capability, and the result would have been the loss of the *CG-40564* and most likely the loss of her three-man crew.

The forty-footers were phased out in the 1970s and were replaced by the faster forty-one footers, which were never accepted well by the men that operated them on the coastal stations. The dislike for them was mainly because they could only be operated from an inside control station. In the early '80s, there was a capsizing of a forty-one-footer on the Columbia River bar resulting in the loss of two men. After this tragedy, forty-one-footers were prohibited from operating in coastal stations and were moved to inland units.

After discussing the good and bad points of the boats used by the Coast Guard on its coastal lifeboat stations during the 1940s-1960s, there is one more item that needs to be added about the thirty-six-foot lifeboats. This would be about its self-righting capabilities.

Its ability to self-right after being capsized to 180 degrees was not only enhanced by the two-ton bronze keel. On the main deck area, there were three watertight structures; each one was built over the forward survivors' compartment, the engine compartment, and the rudder quadrant compartment.

Between these three compartments, there were two self-bailing well decks: one aft where the boat was operated from and the other forward at the entrance to the survivors' compartment. Together, these three compartments provided more than enough buoyancy if the boat were capsized to 180 degrees, along with the two-ton keel, to self-right the boat in a matter of seconds.

CG-40564 as she was 12 January 1961.

4

Most Hazardous

If you go down to the area at the mouth of the Columbia River today and look at the small coastal towns, you will find them much the same as they were fifty years ago. Most of the economy has been drawn from logging, commercial fishing, and cranberries. Willapa Bay also has one of the largest oyster industries on the West Coast. With the decline of the fishery industries in the late 1900s and early part of the new century after 2000, the economy has shifted toward tourism.

Looking at the surnames of those living in this area, you would also find that they were consistent with Scandinavian ancestry. Occupations chosen were handed down to descendants over the years.

The history of the fishing industry can be traced back to when Astoria was the first settlement on the West Coast of the United States. Smaller towns sprouted up around the core area of Astoria such as Warrenton and Hammond on the Oregon side and Chinook and Ilwaco on the Washington side.

When the Lewis and Clark expedition reached the area at the mouth of the Columbia River, they wrote in their diaries about the relentless roar of the pounding surf. They stated that during storms, the noise would be almost intolerable for days on end. This area, in later years, would become known as the Graveyard of the Pacific with the loss of hundreds of boats, ships, and lives.

Of all the occupations found in this area, the fisheries industry has been the most hazardous with many lives lost each year along the West Coast of the United States, especially in the crab fishery. Season wise, the crab fisherman had to work the most hazardous weather and sea conditions, which were in the winter months.

During the winter, the mariner can have calm seas with no wind that changes in a very short period to gale-force winds and twenty- to thirty-foot seas. When these large seas arrived at the shallower waters in the areas of bar entrances and beaches, they could grow in height and break with a tremendous force. Far offshore, storms can contribute to very hazardous bar and ocean conditions.

Most commercial fishing boats are constructed so that they have a very high degree of stability. Hulls are the displacement type with large holds for the catch. Unlike a boat that is built for speed and rides on top of the water, a displacement hull sits very low in the water, and at speed will not lesson its draft. The displacement type of boat, unless altered after construction, is highly survivable in some of the worst conditions while operating in waters of the Pacific Northwest. It is not uncommon today to find many of the wooden boats that were built in the 1920s and '30s still in operation. A lot of them have remained in the same families, being handed down from a parent to a child that most likely had grown up working alongside the parent. As long as the boats maintain their watertight integrity, mechanics are operating properly, and they are in the hands of a skilled operator, they are able to handle very rough sea conditions.

The start of the crab season is usually the most lucrative as higher negotiated prices for the catch are in effect, and the crabs are most abundant. Price and abundance themselves tempt many a fisherman to take chances that they would not normally do.

Each day during the winter months, as far as daylight is concerned, there is only about ten hours of light. Trips have to be planned by the bar, ocean, and tidal conditions, visibility, and near-shore forecasts.

Ideally, if a captain decides to go out, he would want to make his return trip during the flood or top of the flood tide. As far as bar conditions are concerned, this period would be the best time to cross in what might be a marginal condition. Therefore, if conditions on an outgoing tide might be marginal but passable in the early-morning hours, this would most likely be the best time for a captain to make the decision to go out.

However, he could get out, work his pots, and be headed back home under the most favorable sea conditions unless something kicked up during the day. This is not always the case.

Usually the date of the season opening is known several days in advance, and the state fisheries allows the crab boat fleet to set their pots twenty-four hours before opening day. They could go back out on the opening day and pick their pots, or if the weather kicked up, they could, with no problem, leave them to soak for a few days. Depending on the amount of pots owned by a fisherman, the size of his boat, and its capacity for transporting pots, several trips might be required to set all of them.

Once in place and the season opened, ideally the fisherman would pick them every three days or so. If they had enough pots, they could collect them every day if the weather cooperated. Rough sea conditions making the crabbers unable to pick up their pots could cause a boat to lose an entire crab season.

Heavy sea conditions can move the sand on the ocean floor around the pots and can literally bury them, making it impossible to hoist the pot. Retrieving lines might, and do, snap when trying to break pots loose, and then the whole pot is lost. The only alternative is for the crabber to bring out a pump on deck, attach a discharge hose to the pot line, and lower it to the bottom. Once there, the pump is started, and the water washes the sand away from the pot. This process is time-consuming, awkward, and dangerous; but pots are expensive, and many have been retrieved this way and put back to work.

It has been known that in the past years during violent storms out of the Southwest, whole strings of pots that were set off on the South Coast of Washington have been washed ashore. Some would be rolled up en masse and balled up in their retrieving lines. Sometimes these pots would be on the beach as much as twenty miles north of where they had been set. If the fisherman was lucky, he could retrieve his pots on the beach, but many others were lost forever in the ocean.

In addition to the harsh weather conditions during the winter months, those who ventured out had to deal with was the water temperature. The average water temperature in the area during the winter months is forty-five degrees. A person would survive in the water for only a short period. Even if a person was wearing all of the foul-weather gear of the type worn at the time (1961), the cold would very quickly penetrate to the bone. Everyone knew that staying alive or being able to help oneself much after being in the water for periods of over twenty to thirty minutes would be about the maximum time a person could tolerate and still live.

5

Around Lifeboat Stations

To serve the commercial fishing and shipping industries, the U.S. Coast Guard (formerly the Revenue Cutter Service) established, at strategic sites along our coasts, various units for this purpose. From the late 1800s until the present, lifeboat stations, lighthouses, ships, and other aids to navigation have been put in place along the Pacific Northwest coast.

Over the years, the stations did not always remain in their original locations, with some having to be moved because of shifting shorelines. Normally the stations and lighthouses have remained in the same general area as to their original placement.

The first lifesaving station on the Pacific coast with a salaried surfman in charge was built in 1877 at Willapa Bay, which is twenty-five miles north of the Columbia River entrance. In 1882, the first full-time crew for Fort Canby station was established at the mouth of the Columbia River, which later would become known as Cape Disappointment. Across the river at Hammond, Oregon, in 1889, the lifesaving station Point Adams opened. In 1897, the next station to open was Grays Harbor, twenty miles north of Willapa Bay. In 1920, the Cape Disappointment station was relocated from Fort Canby to its present location approximately one-quarter mile south.

Various lifeboats were used, starting with those powered by sail and man. Then in the 1930s, the first motorized thirty-six-foot self-bailing, self-righting boat was put in service at Cape Disappointment. In addition, the first of two fifty-two-foot wooden lifeboats, the *Triumph*, was put into service at Point Adams in 1936. By then almost all of the stations were equipped with the thirty-six-foot MLB; and the second wooden fifty-two footer, the *Invincible*, would arrive at Grays Harbor in 1940.

By January 1961, the lifesaving stations became known as lifeboat stations and then later called Coast Guard stations. Over the years, these stations were involved in the saving of many lives and properties. The rescue attempts carried out by the crews at these stations were not always without the sacrifice of men and boats of the U.S. Coast Guard.

It seemed to be a never-ending process. As long as men and boats went to sea, some would be lost. No matter how well man is at operating his craft, unseen mechanical problems will arise putting his life, boat, or ship in jeopardy. The number one thing that man has to deal with is Mother Nature who always seems to be around and will sometimes deal a deadly blow at a moments notice.

In 1961, the Coast Guard was operating with what by today's standards would be very antiquated boats and equipment. During this period, great things were in the works as far as lifeboats go with the construction of the new forty-four-foot steel lifeboats and the four fifty-two-foot steel lifeboats. One of the fifty-two footers had been delivered to the station at Yaquina Bay, Oregon, in 1956 and another to Grays Harbor in 1960. All of these new boats were powered by twin diesel engines and had a positive self-righting capability. Another positive for the Coast Guard would be in 1964 with the establishment of the Coast Guard air station at Astoria, Oregon. Two amphibious HH-52A helicopters were assigned there. Until then the nearest air station to the Columbia River was at Port Angeles, Washington. It was also around 1964-65 that the first wet suits became available for wear at lifeboat stations. These survival suits were very primitive by standards after the year 2000. They were made of one-quarter-inch rubber and had a top and bottom with boots and a headpiece made of the same material.

The top had a zipper down the front. To be able to get into one of these suits, the interior had to be coated with talcum powder. It was a cumbersome process, but surprisingly once properly on, they offered a great deal of buoyancy and protection from the cold water.

The state-of-the-art improvements that were in the works were not in place in January 1961. What was in place then at the lifeboat stations were the men who were very well trained and were willing to put their lives on the line, if needed.

Almost all lifeboat station personnel from the officer in charge down were enlisted men. A couple of warrant officers were assigned to Grays Harbor and Newport, which were then group offices for the stations in their area. With the exception of the officer in charge who was usually in his late thirties, the rest of the crews were generally under thirty with a few old salts in the crew mix. Each Coast Guard district is divided into groups. These group offices are centrally located within the district and, for the purpose of this book, were on the Washington-Oregon coasts. The group offices of the time were placed in the charge of a warrant officer. His duty was to oversee the overall management of several lifeboat stations, lighthouses, and other small units within his area.

The ratings at lifeboat stations consisted of boatswain mates who would operate the boats, the engineers who would maintain the mechanical parts, and the seamen who would maintain the boats in general. All of these men would act as deckhands on missions and were usually cross-trained in some aspect of the others tasks required in a rescue or other boat operation. It was not uncommon for engineers to be fully qualified boat coxswains as well as the seamen. What was not always looked on favorably was the transfer of a boatswain mate that had served all his time aboard ships to a motor lifeboat station. This was especially true if he was replacing another qualified boatswain mate that had been transferred out to another station. Usually the men that were transferred to lifeboat stations from shipboard duties had very little training in the operation of coastal lifeboats. A considerable amount of time had to be spent in training before a man would be qualified to operate the lifeboats.

In the '50s and '60s, the lifeboat stations were very clannish. Usually being assigned to a lifeboat station and qualified at the job enabled the person to stay at various motor lifeboat stations within a district for almost an entire career. The district would at times transfer the different rates to lighthouse duty within the district while training others that took their places. This way, the district would be able to get their hands on the people and transfer them back to stations, bringing back into lifeboat duty fully qualified as boat crews.

6

11 January 1961

Early in the morning of 11 January 1961, several of the crab fishermen were gathered at the Cottage Bakery in Long Beach, Washington, for a cup of coffee and to swap stories. The ocean and bar conditions had not been favorable for them to go out and work their gear for several days. The outlook for the next few days was not good. Present were Ed Kary, owner of the F/V *Doreen*, his brother, Earnest, and Ed's son, Bud. Also present were Roy Gunnari and his crew from the *Jana-Jo*.

Normally, when the weather had been bad for this long, the fishermen would drive up to North Head Lighthouse to check out the conditions of the ocean and the Peacock Spit. From this vantage point, they had a broad view north and south of the coast, spit areas, and Columbia River bar. They could usually get a good idea if they should attempt to go out. From what they saw that morning, they decided to wait it out another day. It had been blowing out of the SSW(south-southwest) at up to forty-miles an hour for the last few days with seas recorded at the Columbia River Lightship from twelve to sixteen feet.

The Columbia River Lightship was located in a strategic spot southwest of the river entrance. The ship supplied aids to the mariner by showing a rotating light, sounding a foghorn when required, transmitting a homing radio signal, and maintaining her position with a heavy mushroom-type anchor. The longer the wind blew from one general direction, the more the seas would continue to grow in height. At the time, they did not have very accurate forecasts for the weather and sea conditions. What the locals did know was that a storm cell could be generated within a storm that could create very high winds for short periods. When this happened, seas that were already large would be turned into a frothy turmoil and become very dangerous.

On this morning, the rest of the fleet had elected, as the Kary's and the Gunnari's had done, to stay inside awaiting better weather. Later that day, most of them went to the Port of Ilwaco and busied themselves with the upkeep of their boats and gear.

At the Coast Guard Station Cape Disappointment, the men were well into the middle of their winter season duties. There was a crew of seventeen men stationed there with Boatswains Mate Chief Doyle Porter in charge. The station had been there since 1920. There was just barely enough room to berth and feed the amount of people assigned to the station. There also was a small house to quarter the officer in charge and his family. Chief Porter's wife, Peggy, was pregnant with their youngest son and she was due to give birth at any time. Being officer in charge, Chief Porter was assumed to be always on duty unless on authorized leave. He would stick close to the station or within phone contact at all times.

It seemed that the rule for the day at all lifeboat stations was to see how much you could get done with so few people and boats. The cape had three boats assigned to them. These were the utility boats *CG-40564* and *CG-40421* and one lone lifeboat, the *CG-36454*. There was no backup lifeboat. Normally, for a lifeboat station to conduct motor lifeboat drills, there would be a second lifeboat in the area where the drills were being conducted. Perhaps the lifeboats from Point Adams would be asked for, but there is no verification of this. When asked in 2007 why the cape did not have a backup lifeboat, Chief Porter said, "I don't know."

If all three of these boats were underway at the same time with their normal crew of three people, over half of the "stations crew" would be out of the station. In the summer months, these boats were normally underway from daylight to dark as were the boats and crew assigned to Point Adams across the river. To make matters worse, after a long day at sea, the crew had to fill out, post reports, and fuel the boats to get them ready for night duty or the next day. Then there were always the night searches for those boaters that were overdue or that had made it in but did not tell anyone. Many a time, these people would be found at a local watering hole. The Coast Guard crews would both call the bar and ask for the person by name or someone would be sent to check for them.

The Coast Guard personnel generally had a good relationship with the locals and the fishermen. All knew that the Coast Guard was there to help if needed, and more than one beer was shared between all with many a sea story told.

There also were radio and lookout watches that had to be maintained twenty-four hours a day. It had been known that, at times, some of the

Coast Guard boats would get underway with a two-man crew, but this was not the norm.

With Chief Porter, it was—as at all stations—a constant battle for funds and new boats. It did not seem feasible to anyone working there that the crew could be stretched any farther, but the crews performed miracles with what little they had to work with. There was already two of the new fifty-two-foot steel MLBs in the Thirteenth District, and another was slated to take the place of the MLB *Triumph* at Point Adams. There were many a heated conversations on the telephone between Chief Porter and Senior Chief Berto at Point Adams as to where the new boat should be assigned. The subject was also discussed with their supervisors at the group and district offices. There was nothing in writing except that the new boat would be finished in 1961 and delivered sometime and somewhere after that time.

Everyone was under the assumption that it would go to Cape Disappointment. This was really the logical choice as the cape was a couple of miles closer to the Columbia River bar. Chief Porter was aware of this and was constantly working on the problems of getting the channel into Baker Bay dredged deep enough to support larger boats. Cape Disappointment also needed a new boathouse and docks that could accommodate a larger station, crew, and boat compliment. Rumors had floated around the crews on both sides of the river. It was generally agreed in all those informal and rumored discussions that the single station would be Cape Disappointment.

On the hill behind station Cape Disappointment was a lookout tower. It was about a quarter-mile drive or walk to get to the tower. Next to the tower was the Cape Disappointment Lighthouse. Both of these structures were well over three hundred feet above the water, and on a clear day, each structure had a sweeping view of the bar upriver to Astoria, Oregon, and for twenty miles to sea both north and south along the shore. On each side of the river and bar entrance are the notorious Clatsop and Peacock Spits flanking the bar on both sides. Clatsop Spit is located on the Oregon side, north of the south jetty, and extends into the channel to the west and north to the main shipping channel on the bar. Peacock Spit extends from the tip of the north jetty seaward one-mile and north for about two miles.

Inside the tower was a radio receiver tuned to the national distress frequency 2182, binoculars, and a chart of the area laid out on a table. That was about it in 1961. There was not any type of radar or direction-finding equipment installed. These items would have been very important pieces of equipment for a lookout tower to have. An automatic direction finder (ADF), of which there were many available from war surplus aircrafts, could be set to the 2182 frequency; and if a call came in, it could pinpoint the direction relative to the lookout tower. It would have been an invaluable piece of equipment, but for some reason, the Coast Guard resisted (perhaps they were afraid directions would be given) that would make the Coast Guard liable. The lack of ADFs in lookout towers can be directly linked to the loss of life.

A vessel in distress would give the Coast Guard its position; and when the Coast Guard would arrive at that spot, nothing was found, resulting in a time-consuming search. In fact, not one boat assigned to the cape had an ADF installed. Point Adams had two boats with an ADF, and they were the MLB *Triumph* and the *CG-40514*. Throughout the '60s, the ADF in the *CG-40514* was put to good use during the busy summer months.

In 1961, what antiquated equipment the crews had available to take on a boat was the old portable battery-operated RDF (radio direction finder). These had an antenna on top that was turned by hand and attempts were made to get a direction to a vessel in distress. These units were all but useless, and if it was storming out, they were totally useless. Every aircraft flying for the Coast Guard had automatic direction finders in 1961. Why did not all the boats at stations have ADFs? After World War II, there were thousands of them in military aircrafts. Those aircraft were mothballed and later scrapped, and the Coast Guard could have easily used the old ADFs. The few ADFs that the Coast Guard had were the exact same as those used in an aircraft. Someone had to go through the channels to obtain them, and why only a few were procured is unknown.

Cape Disappointment lookout tower 1961.

7

Across the River

Across the bar on the Oregon side and at the back off the beach was a Coast Guard lookout tower that stood about one hundred feet tall. People from Point Adams stood lookout watches in this tower during daylight hours of the summer months. The tower had a great view of the south beach and all of Clatsop Spit. Point Adams at Hammond also had a cubicle tower on top of the main building where the crews stood radio and lookout watches year round.

A crew of twenty-two men and five boats were assigned to the Point Adams station (the MLB *Triumph*, *CG-52301*, *CG-36535*, *CG-36554*, and two utility boats: *CG-40514* and *CG-40416*). At Point Adams, during the busy summer months, it was the same as all lifeboat stations—underway from dawn to dusk with all boats. Point Adams on the Oregon side of the Columbia River entrance was the same as Cape Disappointment on the Washington side—with the crews kept busy with over six hundred calls a year between both of the stations. Also in 1961, the duty at lifeboat stations was port and starboard year-round. The crew went to work at 7:00 AM and did not get off until 5:00 PM the next day. You would have overnight liberty and start the same process the next morning with duty lasting overnight and until 5:00 PM on a rotating basis. Under port and starboard duty, crew members would get a weekend off every other week. This system of duty would get somewhat better in later years with two out of three and three out of four liberty for the higher ratings.

At Point Adams, there was also a large boathouse on the shoreline of the river. The crews could bring three of the boats out of the water on cradles and into the boathouse itself. They would normally, in the winter months, pull out the forty footers and put them inside for annual maintenance. The thirty-six-foot MLBs were left at the docks as backups for Cape Disappointment and, on rotation one at a time, would be taken out of the water for maintenance.

The *Triumph* was also used during the winter months for transporting supplies and crew to and from the Columbia Lightship. This was normally done weekly on Tuesdays and would depart in the early morning. In fact, a trip was scheduled for the morning of 12 January 1961 to transport the new commanding officer, CHBOSN W-2 Ray E. Johnson, out to the ship.

There was room for all the people attached to each station to be housed in the respective station's main building. Married crew members could and often would choose to rent a house in the local community. The married men attached to Cape Disappointment frequently rented homes in Ilwaco or other Long Beach Peninsula communities. Those at Point Adams were likely to rent a home in Hammond or Warrenton, Oregon, for their families.

The MLB *Triumph* (*CG-52301*) and the MLB *Invincible* (*CG-52300*) were the only two of their kind. These two boats had the distinction of being the smallest Coast Guard boats with names. The *Triumph* had one more distinction, and that was a crew from Point Adams went to the East Coast to pick her up at the Coast Guard Yard in Baltimore, Maryland. They brought her all the way around through the Panama Canal. She was and still is the smallest Coast Guard vessel to make such a long journey. This trip was made in 1936 and ended at Point Adams, which at the time was located in a brand new building at Hammond, Oregon. This was a beautiful building then as it remains so today.

One more item needs to be added to the scenery at Point Adams in 1961, and that was the pilot boat, *Peacock*. She was really a small ship belonging to the Columbia River Bar Pilots Association. She was a former 136-foot Navy minesweeper and made of wood. The *Peacock* was named after the legendary Peacock Spit at the mouth of the Columbia and was used in the '50s and '60s to transport bar pilots out to ships across the bar. Once outside the bar, she would meet with these ships at the pilot station near the lightship. When on station, the Peacock would launch a small sturdy rowboat that was used to go alongside the ships. This was very dangerous, but they did it with remarkable skill.

To save time and fuel, the bar pilots moored the *Peacock*, when in port, on the upriver side of the Point Adams boathouse. There was a one-hundred-foot row of pilings with a small walkway coming out from the entrance to the boathouse.

This was very convenient for the pilots as it would save several miles; they would otherwise have to travel by boat. The pilots would either drive their cars out and park at the station or take a taxi out from Astoria. It is not known as to what kind of a relationship the pilots had with the Coast Guard that allowed them to tie up at the station, but this practice was used for several years.

During and after the Second World War, numerous small ships were constructed for the military in shipyards at Tacoma, Washington, and Astoria and Coos Bay, Oregon. The sister ship to the *Peacock* was built at Western Boat in Tacoma.

The *Peacock*'s sister ship was commissioned as the WMS *133* (minesweeper) in 1943. On her maiden voyage south with her Navy crew aboard and because of bad weather, the captain decided to seek refuge in Coos Bay, Oregon. While crossing the bar, things took a turn for the worse, and the captain decided to turn around. While broadside in her turn, a large breaker hit, rolling her over. Along with the ship, thirteen of her crew was lost. A crab boat and a Coast Guard thirty-six-foot MLB picked up the remaining crew members. Both of these boats—with the survivors, and due to conditions on the bar—had to proceed to sea and were unable to return to port until the next day. This event, like so many others in boating history, give yet another reason why the operator of a boat or ship should never put the crew or any passengers and vessel in jeopardy while crossing hazardous bars unless the boat or ship was built specifically for this type of service. Once committed and in the middle of the worst type of conditions, placing the vessel broadside to breaking seas often results in tragedy.

The pilot association did take very good care of the men stationed at Point Adams as far as fishing gear and bait were concerned. In the summer months, if the station had time, they would load up some pilots on the forty-footer, take them out to the *Peacock* and write it off as a training trip. The pilots would reciprocate at times, when they could, by stopping by the lightship to deliver mail and then bring in mail when they returned to port. In general, each group had great respect for the other.

Pilot Boat Peacock as she was in 1961

Coast Guard Station Pt. Adams, Hammond, Oregon, note tower atop building where the crew stood lookout and communication watches.

8

The Men of Point Adams in 1961

Senior Chief Boatswains Mate Warren Berto

Chief Berto was in his early thirties when, in 1959, he had been the officer in charge at Willapa Bay Lifeboat Station. This station was just over twenty miles north of the Columbia River. He had been offered a set of orders for the Dalles, Oregon, which at the time was an aids-to-navigation (ATON) station. He and his wife, Rina, checked it out and found it not to their liking, and instead he accepted a set of orders to Point Adams as the officer in charge. This was a stepping-stone for Chief Berto toward achieving the rank of master chief boatswains mate or accepting a commission as warrant officer. He knew of the station's fine crew and its standing in the local community. During 1960, Chief Berto settled in to the job of commanding the station and men. He and his wife, Rina, like the other young families, rented a home in the area and moved in to raise their two young sons, Warren and Bob. The boys entered the local school in the first and third grades.

Boatswain Mate First Class John L. Culp

BM1 Culp, age thirty-one, was born in Payette, Idaho. He grew up on the family farm along with three brothers and two sisters in Vale, Oregon. At seventeen, John set off to find his niche in life and joined the Army in 1947, leaving the Army in 1948 with an honorable discharge. Culp enlisted in the Army reserves and was again discharged on 18 July 1950. The next day, he signed up with the U.S. Navy. He served a tour as an aviation boatswains mate onboard the aircraft carrier *Coral Sea* and was honorably discharged on 19 April 1954. There were a couple of years between 1954 and 1956 that Culp was not a member of any armed forces.

In 1956, he again enlisted; and this time, he went into the U.S. Coast Guard as a seaman. Because he had prior service, the only boot camp Culp had to attend was the shorter orientation version at Alameda, California. He served onboard a couple of ships and, on 21 October 1957, ended up on the CG Cutter *Winona* at Port Angeles, Washington. By that time, he had thought that he had finally found a home and set to work on becoming a boatswain's mate.

He worked hard, took out the required courses, and became a seaman boatswains mate striker. The *Winona* was a patrol cutter that would go on lengthy operations in the North Pacific. When in port, the crew would hang out at the local watering holes and partake in the many recreational activities that the local area offered.

One day Culp went on an outing to a park lookout outside of Port Angeles, and there he just happened to meet his future wife, LaVerne Kesler.

On 1 March 1958, John L. Culp and LaVerne were married at Port Angeles, Washington; and in December, Culp got a set of orders to the Lifeboat Station Point Adams at Hammond, Oregon. LaVerne stayed back in Port Angeles and worked for a few months to help scrape together some money to help in finding a home to rent in Hammond. Soon after arriving at Point Adams, Culp got his promotion to boatswains mate third class. Within just a couple of years, he would be promoted to boatswains mate first class. LaVerne had joined him, and they settled down to start a family. It seemed that after all of those years roaming around the military, Culp had finally found what he was looking for. His son, John Lee Culp II, was born in May of 1959, and daughter Cheryl followed in October 1960. He had his career, a wife, and two children whom he and LaVerne had brought into the world and whom they dearly loved.

Culp could be a little rough around the edges when dealing with people. This could have been due to his Dutch-German descent. He could be stubborn and persistent at times, and during his career in the Coast Guard, this would be to his advantage. It would be the driving force that got him to continue no matter what the situation was.

Boatswain Mate First Class John C. Webb

BM1 Webb, although not attached to Point Adams in January 1961, had been transferred to North Head Light Station at Ilwaco, Washington.

When he was old enough, he joined the Coast Guard; and out of boot camp, he was sent as a seaman to Point Adams in 1957. By 1960, he had been promoted to the rank of BM1.

During this period, he had met and married his wife, Vallory; and by 1960, they had two daughters, Terry and Brenda. Duty at lifeboats stations can be very hectic and dangerous at times. Webb had been raised in the Astoria area, and his family was involved in the fisheries industry. Webb's father, Jack, operated a crab boat out of Warrenton, Oregon.

Webb jumped at the chance when an opening came up to be officer in charge at North Head Light Station. This type of duty was kind of laid-back and did not require the high-energy output of the men that lifeboat duty did. Webb would take his young family there so he could spend more time with them. One other benefit was that, by living in government quarters, there was a possibility by close management that the Webb's could save some money.

Boatswain Mate First Class Hernando Lopez

When BM1 Webb transferred to North Head in 1960, it left an opening at Point Adams. Hernando Lopez was a BM1 attached to a buoy tender at Astoria, and he received a set of orders for Point Adams. Lopez had been in the Coast Guard for several years, and most of that time, he had been on seagoing units, mainly buoy tenders. He had originally been a damage control man with the rank of DC first class. He had a strong interest in the boatswain mate rate, and since it was allowed to lateral over between damage control man and boatswain mate at the time, he finished the required courses and became a BM1. Other than operating the ship's small boats, he had absolutely no experience on lifeboats. At the time the orders came in, Lopez was ready to try something new.

From the minute he reported to Point Adams, he was welcomed aboard, but he got the feeling that he did not really fit in with this bunch of crew members. It really was an entirely different Coast Guard than what he had become used to in other places. Over the next several months, he did his best to fit in. He knew his rate well other than situations around lifeboats. The station had drills on the boats all the time that gave him the opportunity to learn what was expected of him. There were always plenty of calls to go on as a trainee, but it would take time to learn what it had taken others years to do.

Boatswain Mate First Class Willis P. Miller

BM1 Miller was born at the Swedish Medical Center in Seattle, Washington, on 20 June 1935. He was raised in what is now known as the city of Shoreline. Miller was always called by his middle name, Paul, and never had a problem with this until he entered the Coast Guard and had to produce documentation. On official records, he was thereafter Willis P. Miller but always answered to the name Paul.

Miller attended Lincoln High School in Seattle, Washington, graduating in 1953; and then there was a short stay at the Seattle University. His grade average was not up to par, and since the draft was still in effect, he decided that maybe he should enter the military branch of his own choice. He and a friend had gone together and joined the Marines. When Miller told his dad that he was going to be a Marine, his dad objected and encouraged Miller to change over to the Coast Guard.

Miller entered the Coast Guard on 12 November 1954 and spent two months in boot camp at Alameda, California. Like most of the others, after attending boot camp on the West Coast, he was sent to Coast Guard Base Seattle. He had a short stay there until he was assigned to the buoy tender *Fir* as a seaman apprentice.

Miller stayed onboard the *Fir* for the next four years, rising to the rank of first class boatswains mate by the end of his enlistment. Making first class in four years was quite an accomplishment. Those who made this type of advancement in their first enlistment were referred to as slick-armed first class. This designation meant that the individual had not yet earned the hash mark for their left arm that signified they had served four years. Hash marks are given for every four years of completed service.

Miller had met his future wife, Joan, while in middle school at Richmond Beach (now a part of Shoreline, Washington). They had both been raised in this area but did not start dating until May of 1954. Miller was attending school at Seattle University, and Joan was a senior in high school.

On 1 October 1955, Miller and Joan were married, and by then, he was a third class boatswains mate on the *Fir*. Most military wives, when not raising children, would hold down jobs to bring in extra income to make ends meet. Joan held a job at Pacific Tel. and Tel. until close to the time their first child, Dan, was born in June 1957.

In November 1959, Miller was assigned to Point Adams Lifeboat Station at Hammond, Oregon. The young family soon found a home to rent a short distance from the station. For the next year, Miller would busy himself with learning the area and operations of the boats and station.

Boatswain Mate Second Class John S. Hoban

BM2 Hoban was born in 1933 at Independence, Missouri. Not much is known about Hoban's earlier life before joining the Coast Guard. It is known that Hoban ended up as a boatswains mate third or second class at the captain of the port moorings in Astoria, Oregon.

The duties there included security of the port, boarding, inspecting, and identifying ships entering the Columbia River on their way to inland ports. The unit would close down in 1960 with the men being transferred to other ships and stations in the area. While stationed there, Hoban would observe the boats from Point Adams underway on search-and-rescue missions. Rather than wait for the Coast Guard to send him to a ship, he put in for a transfer to Point Adams in 1960. When Hoban arrived at Point Adams, he brought with him his young wife, Judy; and they set up housekeeping in a rental house at Hammond, Oregon. He was placed into a training program on the boats to qualify as coxswain. Although Hoban was an experienced boat operator for the forty-foot utility boats, the operations at the port security unit did not involve the use of lifeboats or operations in the open ocean and on the bar area.

Engineman Third Class Joseph E. Petrin

EN3 Petrin was born in Port Angeles, Washington, and graduated from Renton High School in Renton, Washington. Petrin joined the Coast Guard in 1957, and after boot camp, he was first assigned to the Coast Guard Cutter *Wachusett* based out of Seattle, Washington. It was not long after that he was transferred to the Coast Guard Cutter *Northwind* in the fall of 1958. He was just in time to leave on the *Northwind's* trip to the Antarctic in support of Operation Deep Freeze IV. In 1959, there was a five-month trip on the ship to Alaska on a medical-dental mission to villages on the Alaska coasts as far north as the Arctic Circle. During this period, Joe's duties were with the ships engineering department. He became an engineering striker up for third class, which he would be advanced to in 1959.

After the two trips on the *Northwind*, Petrin heard about an opening for a third class engineer at Lifeboat Station Point Adams in Hammond, Oregon. He would still be close to home so Petrin applied for the transfer and was accepted. He arrived at Point Adams in January 1960 and immersed himself in learning the engineering aspects of all the boats assigned to the station.

Engineman Third Class Gordon Huggins

EN3 Huggins went into the Coast Guard in 1958. He had thought that this would be a good opportunity for a career and anticipated a twenty-year tour. After boot camp, he was sent to Groton, Connecticut, to attend radio school. Huggins said that he did not get along well with the dots and dashes of Morse code, so he was sent out to Base Seattle in the Thirteenth District as a seaman.

While in Seattle, Huggins had gotten married to his wife, Patricia. In the Thirteenth District, they had several semi-isolated light stations where you could have your family with you as long as there were not any school-age children. Huggins put in for one of these stations and received orders for Destruction Island, which was two and a half miles off the Washington coast and about sixteen miles south of La Push, Washington. This was, in reality, the most isolated family station in the district. In a storm, there was absolutely no way on or off the island.

After a year and a half, with periodic breaks from the island, Huggins was transferred to the Captain of the Port, Portland, Oregon. He was a crewmember on one of the forty-foot patrol boats. In the busy summer months, this boat and crew were sent down to Point Adams to assist the station with their patrol duties.

Huggins liked Point Adams and the area so when he got back to Portland, he requested a full-time assignment to the lifeboat station. He received a set of orders on 1 December 1960. He left his wife in Vancouver, Washington, until he could get situated in Hammond.

Seaman Boatswains Mate Ralph Mace

SNBM Mace was born in Seattle, Washington, in 1941 and was raised in the area. He graduated from high school on Vashon Island, Washington. He joined the Coast Guard in February 1959 and attended boot camp at Alameda, California. After boot camp, Mace went to Base Seattle for further transfer as a seaman apprentice to Point Adams. He liked lifeboat station duty, especially the part about being a boatswains mate. After making seaman, he took whatever courses were available and became a seaman boatswain mate striker.

Becoming a striker meant that he would have the added responsibilities of leading work details and would be trained in the operation of all the boats. In other words, he would be taken under the wing of a more senior boatswains mate. Before making third class, he would be qualified in the operation of one or more of the station's boats. Until then he would act as a seaman onboard the boats.

Seaman Gordon Sussex

Sussex was raised in Bellevue, Washington. He graduated from Bellevue High School and attended Everett Junior College and the University of Washington for a while. Sussex had a twin sister, Gwen, and they were very close. He had a lifelong dream of joining the U.S. Coast Guard, but a years-long battle with a kidney disorder prevented him from enlisting. He had been in and out of the hospital and under a doctor's care for many years.

While attending college, Sussex had tests done on a regular basis to monitor his condition. After a period of time, the tests showed everything had stabilized; he got this in writing from his physicians and headed to the Coast Guard recruiting office. He was accepted and joined on 21 March 1960 and was sent for a three-month tour of boot camp at Alameda, California. After Sussex graduated, he—like so many others—ended up at Base Seattle. The base was the staging area for transferring men to wherever they might be needed within the Thirteenth District. Sussex was hoping that he would not get orders to a ship, and his wish came true when he was sent to the lifeboat station at Point Adams.

He would be close to home for short visits and, at the same time, be around boats and the water, which he loved. It later would be found that Sussex had licked one ailment to only acquire another. He had chronic seasickness.

Some people never get seasick, and some that do get over it. Then there is chronic seasickness, which can completely incapacitate a person. After arriving at Point Adams, Seaman Sussex worked right into the routine, and he excelled at doing so. However, his first boat ride into the ocean did not go so well for him. He had never before been in the ocean where there had been long rolling swells and the smell of diesel smoke that in combination had made many men very sick. Sussex had not counted on this and had hoped that it would be a passing thing. He took all the kidding from others and tried to go on every boat call that he could, hoping that he would get over his horrible tendency to get seasick.

The Local People of Hammond, Oregon

As stated before, the small communities at the mouth to the Columbia River were all very close knit. Colleen Simonsen and her husband, Howard, were two civilians in Hammond that had close relationships with most of the men and families at Point Adams. Howard was a volunteer firefighter for the town of Hammond, and Colleen served with the women's auxiliary for the Hammond fire department. It was through this organization, in particular, that Colleen formed friendships and, in some cases, lifelong bonds with some of the Coast Guard wives. Many of the Point Adams men were volunteer firefighters, and the wives were members of the auxiliary. Colleen did not have a problem with getting close to the Coast Guard wives; perhaps it was because she was a few years older than the average age of most of the wives. The whole community had a close bond with the motor lifeboat *Triumph* dating back to 1936 when the boat was brought around to Point Adams via the Panama Canal. They considered the *Triumph* as something that belongs to them. In fact, there were several local men, two of whom were Arley Jensen and Don Shaw, who had served in the Coast Guard and had been assigned to Point Adams years before. Jensen had been an engineer onboard the *Triumph* throughout the Second World War years and later retired from the Coast Guard to reside in Hammond. Don Shaw had been a seaman on the *Triumph* during the war years and owned Shaw's Market in Hammond.

9

The Men of Cape Disappointment in 1961

Boatswains Mate Chief Doyle S. Porter

Porter joined the U.S. Coast Guard at Mayport, Florida, in 1947 and spent his first three years onboard the 250-foot cutter *Macoma*. While on the *Macoma*, Porter was advanced from seaman to third class boatswains mate. He later transferred to the Coast Guard Cutter *Bering Strait* where he made second and then first class. Porter transferred to the patrol boat *CG-83481* where he was promoted to chief and then assigned as officer in charge of the *CG-83453*.

Toward the end of the fifties, Chief Porter was sent on a mission down the coast of Oregon to look around and recommend the establishment and placement of any new lifeboat stations. In 1957, Chief Porter was assigned as the officer in charge of lifeboat station Cape Disappointment, Ilwaco, Washington.

At the time, it was a small station with three boats and twelve men assigned to the station. Porter and his wife, Peggy, would reside at the cape from 1957 to 1963. Chief Porter made many improvements that would make the station what it is today.

Engineman Second Class Terrance Lowe

Lowe was born on 11 June 1940 and raised in the Seattle, Washington, area. While growing up, Lowe—off and on, from the age of twelve—worked at one of his dad's service stations. These duties, in addition to doing well at Snohomish High School, gave him the work ethics and drive to do well in his future life.

During his junior and senior years, he would work the 4:00 PM to midnight shift at one of the service stations, six days a week. It was while at work one evening that he observed the Coast Guard boats on patrol in Elliot Bay. He thought that this type of work was something that could really be of interest to him.

After graduating from high school, he went to the Coast Guard recruiters' office and signed up. He went to boot camp in August of 1958 at Alameda, California. Due to his mechanical background from working at the service stations, Lowe came out of boot camp as a fireman apprentice, one of the many career steps for his future.

He was sent to Base Seattle to await further transfer to one of the district's units or ships. He was soon sent to the *Swiftsure* Lightship located at the Swiftsure Bank off the entrance to the Strait of Juan de Fuca. He stayed on the *Swiftsure* for twenty-six months where the crew would spend six weeks aboard and then have two weeks off. This was sedentary duty so there was recreational equipment onboard to allow the crew to get some needed exercise. Lowe heavily used the weight lifting and exercise equipment. He was a small man by stature, but by the time his tour on the lightship was up, he was in great physical shape—something that along with his work ethic would lead to his survival in the near future.

During his two years onboard the *Swiftsure*, Lowe had been advanced to engineman second class. In 1960, he was assigned as a second class to the lifeboat station at Cape Disappointment.

Seaman Apprentice Acie Maxwell

Maxwell was born in Kansas City, Missouri, and raised from childhood in Kent, Washington. He graduated from Kent Meridian High School in 1959. His father encouraged him to join the Coast Guard, and in 1959, Maxwell went to boot camp at Alameda, California. After boot camp, Maxwell stayed an additional six months at Alameda playing brass instruments in the Coast Guard band. He was then transferred to Base Seattle to await orders.

Maxwell's orders came in May of 1960. He transferred as a seaman apprentice to Coast Guard Station Cape Disappointment. His duties at the cape started with the maintenance of the station and boats. He was also a deckhand on the vessels assigned to the station.

Seaman Apprentice James L. Crocker

Crocker was born 15 March 1942, at Salem, Oregon. He spent his pre-high school years there. His family then moved to the Seattle area where he attended Franklin High School. Like some others in those late teenage years, he was at the point of getting into trouble if he did not change his ways. His aunt told him that maybe he should enlist in the service, and for some unknown reason, Crocker's aunt suggested the Coast Guard.

In the spring of 1960, soon after he reached his eighteenth birthday, he entered the Coast Guard and was off to boot camp in Alameda. Instead of the normal twelve weeks of boot training, Jim spent almost sixteen weeks there. When he had arrived at Alameda, he was put into what was called a forming company until they had enough men to make up a full company. When he graduated from boot camp, he received a set of orders that sent him to the Lifeboat Station Cape Disappointment, Ilwaco, Washington, as a seaman apprentice.

First Class Boatswains Mate Darrell Murray

Murray was raised in the Montana area and joined the Coast Guard in 1953. He served some time on the *Relief* Lightship out of Seattle and then a tour at Lifeboat Station Neah Bay. He was transferred to Cape Disappointment in 1958, rising to the rank of boatswain mate first class.

Murray's duties at the cape were to supervise the deck personnel under him in the maintenance and operation of the station and boats. This also included the operation of the station boats under all conditions and any duties required in the saving of life and property at sea and ashore. The performance of these duties would give Murray a great sense of accomplishment.

Fireman-Engineer Brian Johnson

Johnson arrived at Cape Disappointment from a light station in the Puget Sound area in the summer of 1960. He had been raised in Astoria, Oregon, and graduated from Astoria High School in 1957. For a short period, he attended Oregon Institute of Technology and then returned to the coastal areas of Washington State by enlisting in the U.S. Coast Guard. To Johnson, this was the duty he had always wanted. He could make regular trips across the river to visit friends and family.

Seaman Boatswain Mate Larry Edwards

Edwards was raised in the Yakima, Washington, area and joined the Coast Guard Reserve in 1959. After boot camp, he was assigned to Heceta

Head Lighthouse in Oregon. At Heceta Head, he would choose his career in the Coast Guard, and that was to be a boatswain mate.

In 1960, he was transferred to Cape Disappointment as a seaman boatswains mate where he remained until 1963. While stationed at the cape, he learned leadership skills and the operation of the station boats.

10

Early 12 January 1961

Between 5:00 AM and 6:00 AM, the crabbers from Ilwaco gathered at the local coffee shops to discuss the possibility of getting out on the morning of 12 January 1961. The tide had been on the flood with high water on the bar at around 8:00 AM. Ed, Earnest, and Bud Kary of the crab boat *Doreen* had been up to North Head Lighthouse. They informed the other crabbers over coffee that it did not look very promising for them to go out that morning, and that they had decided to stay in for another day or so.

Most of the fishermen were anxious to get out and pick their pots, rebait, and set them out again. During heavy sea conditions, pots left down for long periods had a tendency to sand in. The only boats electing to go out that morning were the *Jana-Jo* skippered by Roy E. Gunnari and the *Mermaid*, owned and operated by Bert Bergman and his brother, Stanley, of Chinook, Washington.

The *Mermaid* was a thirty-eight-foot double-ended boat that the brothers had purchased the year before for around $12,000. They had been in the crab fishery for only a few years. Roy Gunnari was the more experienced of the two. As for the *Jana-Jo*, she was a very well-built wood commercial fishing boat of around forty-five feet long.

In an interview with Myrtle Kary years later, she stated that Bert Bergman's attitude of being somewhat invincible was not a trait that he had alone. This invincible attitude with a strong sense of daring against the elements of nature was characteristics held by many fishermen and by operators of the Coast Guard boats that one day might go to their rescue. Being a fisherman requires that, at times in order to make a living, the fisherman would operate on the very edge of conditions that could do them harm. The boats used were generally well maintained and were usually well suited to most conditions where the fisherman would operate. Should there be equipment failure and marginal sea conditions, they could be put in immediate peril. Sometimes making a living was hard due to adverse weather and poor fishing or crabbing. Then it was more likely that the care of the boat and its mechanics might be neglected.

For boats at sea in and around crab pot areas, hazards can be encountered where the lines and buoys go to the pot. Normally, the crab pot buoys and some line float on the surface. Under certain conditions, these buoys are drug under the surface by the current becoming invisible to other boaters. Any boats operating in the area run the chance of traveling over these unseen lines and fouling their propellers. To counter this possible problem, most fishing boats were built with the prop enclosed within a shoe that ran aft from the keel with the bottom of the rudder resting in the shoe. With that safeguard in place on most of the boats, a line caught by the boat would be deflected away from the propeller and exit past the stern.

As for the Coast Guard boats, the thirty-six-foot lifeboats were built as described in previous chapters. If needed, these boats could operate in the shallows and surf where crab pot lines might be located. However, even with the propeller guards in place, this device did not always keep the crab pot lines out of propellers.

The Coast Guard forty-footer was a utility boat and was built for speed at an average of twenty knots. This speed was helpful in getting to a boater in distress fast in order to get them out of immediate trouble. The forty-footers had both screws hanging off the shaft supported by struts and a shaft bearing. The boats were very vulnerable to getting lines in the props and hung up on the rudders. When the forty-footers had to operate in crab pot areas, and especially at night, certain measures were taken to prevent fouling of the propellers. The coxswain would keep an eye out for crab pot lines while operating the boat at high RPMs until they reached the boat needing assistance. Traveling at this speed and in this manner would often avoid fouling the propellers or rudders with crab pot line as the line would travel along the keel and out the back.

If a line did get into the propeller, the sharp propeller turning at high speed would cut the line. When taking a boat in tow in a crab pot area, the forty footers became more vulnerable to snagging a crab pot line when traveling at only seven to eight knots. Getting lines in propellers could cause a forty-footer to become a victim along with the boat and people it had been sent to rescue.

When a call came into the Coast Guard to go to the aid of a disabled boat, careful consideration in choosing which rescue boat to use needed to be taken.

Before 12 January 1961, it had been uneventful at Point Adams. At 6:00 AM, reveille had been made for the men, and they were out of bed getting ready for breakfast. Around this same time, similar things were happening at Cape Disappointment station. The *Jana-Jo* and *Mermaid* were passing the station on their way to the Columbia River entrance.

At 7:00 AM, liberty was up at Point Adams, and the men that had been off the night before were trickling in for breakfast. Each station had an allowance per man for meals, and to save money, that would be spent at home for food; the men would eat at the station as much as possible.

A logistics run to the lightship was planned for the morning to transport supplies and the new commanding officer, CWO-W2 Ray E. Johnson, out to the ship. The motor lifeboat *Triumph* was the boat chosen for this run, and the men that were going had eaten breakfast early. They had gone to the mooring basin to load the provisions onboard that were brought to the dock by local distributors. There was really no place on the outside deck to stow things, so everything had to be taken down below into the forward compartment.

Everything that would provide the lightship crew in the way of food, movies, and personnel were taken on these weekly trips, weather permitting. No matter what the sea conditions at the lightship were, it seemed that on crew-change days, the ship would say that they had a light swell and light winds. The men on the lightship stayed onboard for six weeks and then were off for two. They were always anxious to get ashore when their time was due. The stations that supplied these ships were well aware that the weather reports on these days were often downplayed by as much as 50 percent. Observations from both the pilot boat, if on station, and Cape Disappointment lookout tower would be used for the decision to make the run or not.

The lightship normally rode at anchor with her bow into the weather and seas. In fact, with plenty of fenders out from the ship and supply boat and once lines were passed, the supply boat would ride safely in rather large seas. The primary concern for the coxswain was the conditions on the bar. Before leaving the station, he would again contact the pilot boat and the lookout tower at Cape Disappointment. The most reliable information would be from the pilot boat as the tower at the cape was over 150 feet above the water, and a true measure of the seas could not be made. Generally, if possible, a tie-up alongside the lightship would be attempted; and the mission completed.

During the two days before 12 January, the weather and sea conditions had been marginal for resupplying with seas up to twelve feet. Winds had been out of the southwest at twenty to thirty knots with higher gusts to forty knots at times. That morning, all reports that Point Adams received were showing that conditions from the pilot boat and the cape's tower were a go for the trip.

It was 8:00 AM as the *Triumph* departed the Hammond mooring basin and entered the Columbia River outbound toward the bar. Conditions on the river were calm with visibility of around eight miles. The *Triumph* crossed the bar at high-water slack. The trip would be uneventful, and while crossing the bar and heading toward the lightship, the F/V *Jana-Jo* and *Mermaid* were well into picking their crab pots north of the river mouth.

At 9:45 AM, the *Triumph* arrived alongside the lightship, passed lines, and prepared to off-load passengers and supplies. Below, seamen Ted Ritola and Doug Ponton were handing up boxes and mailbags. This was one job not relished as it was confining and warm due to the engine heat generated below. The heat along with the motion of the boat would make one's mouth water with the first symptoms of seasickness. Thankfully, they had a light load of supplies, and shortly everything was handed topside, and they both leapt at the chance of some fresh air. It was a quick stop at the lightship. With the new commanding officer placed onboard the lightship and the supplies off-loaded, the *Triumph* left the lightship at 10:00 AM and headed back to Point Adams station.

The *Triumph* started her crossing inbound on the bar at around 10:45 AM. She was pushing against a small ebb current, and sea conditions on the bar were swells out of the west at six to eight feet. Visibility was eight miles, and winds were light. Compared to what it would be like on the bar and at sea six to eight hours later, the bar was like a lake. At 11:30 AM, the *Triumph* passed the Fort Stevens light and rounded the corner into the Hammond mooring basin. The crew tied her up at the Coast Guard docks and readied her for her next call before heading for lunch.

Across the river at Cape Disappointment, it also was a routine start to the day. The man in the lookout tower had earlier watched the crabbers and the *Triumph* make their way outbound. As soon as he picked up the *Triumph* making her way down the red buoy line from the lightship, he followed her across the bar and up the river. In the afternoon, Chief Porter made his way to the hospital in Ilwaco where his wife, Peggy, had just given birth to their youngest son, Roy. Things were peaceful at the station, and he had left word with the officer of the deck (OOD), Boatswain Mate First Class Murray, to call him at the hospital if anything came up.

Engineman Third Class Junior Meyer and his wife, Evelyn, paid a visit to the Point Adams station. Meyer and his family were heading toward the ferry that was due to leave at 6:30 PM from Astoria, Oregon, to the Megler Landing on the Washington side of the Columbia. Meyer had been stationed at Point Adams in 1960 when the terms of his enlistment expired, and he had decided not to reenlist in the Coast Guard. While a civilian, one of his children became very ill, resulting in major medical expenses that he and his wife, Evelyn, could not afford.

To help his family out, Meyer applied to the Coast Guard to reenter the service and was accepted at his old rate and rank. There was an opening for an engineer at North Head Lighthouse on the Washington side close to Cape Disappointment. From North Head, the family had access to medical care at the local hospitals and the Madigan Army Hospital at Fort Lewis near Tacoma, Washington.

The Meyers were heading to North Head, and he had stopped by Point Adams for a short visit with old shipmates who were still there including BM1 John Culp. Meyer and Culp had been on many calls together in the past. Culp used to call Meyer, June for short, in a kidding sort of way. While Meyer made a quick run into the station, he left his wife, Evelyn in the warm car.

It had been late afternoon when Chief Berto told BM2 Ronald Brooks to go home to be with his wife, Lois. Lois and Ron had just lost a baby, and Lois came home from the hospital that day. Chief Berto, on the outside, was the boatswain mate-type who seemed gruff and stern when needed but compassionate on the inside. Both Chief Berto and Chief Porter cared greatly about the welfare of the men who served under them, and this concern included their families. Brooks had the duty that day but was told someone would cover for him.

Fishing boat Jana-Jo 1961. The F/V Mermaid was somewhat smaller but just as ruggedly built. No suitable picture of the Mermaid can be found.

CG-40416 from Pt. Adams fueling at the Pt. boathouse. This boat is similar to the CG-40564. Even though these boats performed in many rescues you can see that they would have limited sea keeping abilities.

11

Afternoon 12 January 1961

At around 3:00 PM, Roy Gunnari, onboard the *Jana-Jo* had, been talking to the Bergman's aboard the *Mermaid* on frequency 2638. The 2638 was a working AM radio frequency that was to be used by military and civilian boats and ships only. Land-based radios did not have this frequency. Other frequencies used were the calling and distress frequency 2182 and 2670, which were Coast Guard working frequencies that was used between Coast Guard boats and stations only. They had been discussing how the day had gone, and Roy stated that he was going to head home. The *Mermaid* had just finished picking their pots and was a couple miles north of the *Jana-Jo*. Roy had earlier been keeping an eye on his barometer and had noticed there had been a drop in pressure of twenty points in a short period of time. Roy was an experienced fisherman and was well aware that rapid drops in barometric pressure could mean that some bad weather was coming. Roy said he was heading toward the bar, and Bert said they were doing the same. The *Jana-Jo* came around Peacock Spit between buoys 7 and 9, and Roy looked to see where the best route over the bar and into the river might be. He could see that the middle ground between the black buoy line and the north jetty was rather nasty. It was difficult to judge the true conditions while looking at the back of the swells. He decided that the best route for him was right down the black line to buoy number 11 and the entrance to Baker Bay channel to his moorage at Ilwaco. The tide was now on the flood, and he would get a little extra push going upriver and across the bar.

The *Jana-Jo* had made good time when at 3:30 PM, while making the turn into Baker Bay channel, she received a call on the working frequency 2638 from the *Mermaid*. Bert Bergman was on the radio and told Roy that he was having steering problems. He said his position was at the southwest edge of the shallow waters of Peacock Spit, and he was drifting north across the outer edge of the spit. Bert reported that he still had power but was limited in maneuvering without the rudder. He could not find any obvious problems with the rudder that they could fix.

Bert asked Roy if he would call the Coast Guard for him. It is unknown why the *Mermaid* did not call the Coast Guard on 2182, the national distress frequency, which the *Mermaid* was known to have. Perhaps the Bergmans thought that with the *Jana-Jo* close enough, Roy would come and throw them a line. Normally, fishing boats are not equipped to tow other boats except in ideal conditions, but it has been known to happen. Roy had just crossed the bar and knew it would be advisable to let the better-equipped Coast Guard do the job. Roy switched channels to frequency 2182 and called the cape. Seaman Acie Maxwell was on watch in the cape's tower and took the information from the *Jana-Jo*. Maxwell was just finishing the noon to 4:00 PM lookout watch and would soon be relieved.

Maxwell picked up the phone and called down to the station to alert them. Roy called the *Mermaid* back and told Bert that he had relayed the information to the Coast Guard. For some reason, the cape did not have the *Jana-Jo* tell the *Mermaid* to answer up on 2182. At 3:45 PM, Seaman Dave Trujillo arrived at the Cape tower to relieve the watch from Seaman Maxwell as did Seaman Gordon Sussex relieve the watch in Point Adams tower. Both new lookouts exchanged information and relieved the watch. Maxwell told Trujillo that he had just relayed the information about the *Jana-Jo* and *Mermaid* to the officer of the day, BM1 Darrel Murray. The *Jana-Jo* continued up Baker Bay channel toward her berth at Ilwaco.

The land-based Coast Guard stations were not allowed to have commercial working frequencies like 2638 and 2738. It was some kind of FCC regulation. All the Coast Guard boats did have these frequencies, but it was always confusing getting the boats on the right frequency together. With a lot of switching around, there was always the possibility of losing a connection at a vital time, and the shore stations would be unable to overhear the conversations between the Coast Guard boats and vessels in distress. It was a simple procedure to switch channels. There was a round knob with a pointer on it, and all one had to do to switch channels was to turn the knob with the pointer directed toward the channel selected that was written on a plate beneath the knob. There was a separate knob for volume.

Murray had told Maxwell to hurry down to the station as soon as he was relieved, and that maybe Maxwell would be going with him on this call. Seaman Trujillo settled down in the watch stander's chair and started scanning the area where the *Mermaid* was said to be located, but due to weather conditions, he could not see a thing. The wind was blowing out of the south-southeast at twenty-eight to thirty-three knots or a near gale, raining off and on with visibility down to one to two miles when Trujillo relieved the watch. Now Trujillo was looking down at the bar and trying to judge the conditions. The tower was over 150 feet above the water, and at times when looking down, it was difficult to be very accurate. There were some large swells running across the bar and up the channel. It was the same in the area under the tower with the exception that some looked like they had a little white water on top.

Electronics technician Don Davis was in the cape's boathouse taking an inventory of spare parts. He had earlier gone through all the electronics on the boats and found them in good working order.

At 3:45 PM, the *Jana-Jo* had made her way in and past the Coast Guard boathouse that was located on the west side of Baker Bay channel. Roy stated that he never saw any other boats underway. From the time he was at jetty A and had relayed the distress call, it only took the *Jana-Jo* about fifteen minutes to cover the distance from the entrance to Baker Bay to just past the boathouse.

BM1 Murray grabbed the keys to one of the station's vehicles and drove up the road to the tower. When he entered the tower, he only remained for a couple of minutes after observing what little he could see. Certainly, he had to feel the bite of the wind when he got out of the vehicle, but nonetheless, he had elected to take the utility boat *CG-40564* so he could get to the *Mermaid* faster. He hurried back down the hill, entered the station, and found Engineer Second Class Terry Lowe and Seaman Maxwell. He told them to grab their gear and get in the carryall. He knew Don Davis was at the boathouse, and he made a quick call to make sure that the electronics in the boats were working. Davis told him everything was okay and hung up the phone to continue working. It is not known why Murray did not instruct Trujillo to try to call the *Jana-Jo* when Murray was in the tower or to have Roy get the *Mermaid* to come up on 2182 kc/s. Perhaps in his haste to get assistance to the *Mermaid* started, he never thought to do so.

It may have been possible that the watch stander could then have received vital information, such as an updated position, if the *Mermaid* had been contacted. Possibly Murray could have had the tower watch stander relay such information as asking the *Mermaid* to drop an anchor to keep her from drifting into more dangerous waters. If this had been done, then once the Coast Guard boat got underway, Murray would have had direct communications with the *Mermaid*. For some unknown reason at the start, the *Mermaid* was not contacted directly by the Coast Guard.

Murray picked Seaman Boatswains Mate Larry Edwards to coxswain the backup boat, the motor lifeboat *CG-36454*. This boat would act as a backup in case something might happen to the *CG-40564* that would make the forty-foot boat unable to complete her mission. He quickly found Fireman Brian Johnson and Seaman Apprentice James Croker to fill out the crew. He told them to get their gear and follow the forty-footer as soon as they could. Before leaving the building, he asked someone to call the hospital and let Chief Porter know what was going on.

At the boathouse, the phone rang again; but this time, it was from the tower for Don Davis. Trujillo was required to monitor the three to four radio beacons along the coast as one of his several duties. These radio signals were sent by the respective beacons in sequence to aid the mariner in obtaining the position of his vessel. He informed Davis that the cape's signal seemed to be out of synchronization with the Willapa Bay signal. Davis told him he would be up shortly to fix the problem, hung up the phone, and put his equipment away. The boathouse door opened, and three men came rushing in and proceeded to start the forty-footer and prepare to get underway. Davis did not exchange any words that he remembered with the crew, and he headed out the door. As Davis walked to his jeep, he noted the time was 4:29 PM, and he heard the exhaust noise from the forty-footer as it left the boathouse. The carryall blocked in Davis's jeep, and as the crew had left the keys in it, he took it to the tower leaving the keys of the jeep in the ignition.

It is not known exactly when the thirty-six footer departed. The assistance reports filed later state that they both departed at the same time, which was 4:20 PM. It is known however that the reports are not correct as Davis was at the boathouse when the forty-footer departed, and he did not see anyone else on his way back to the station.

It did not take Davis long to fix the radio beacon sequence, and he was soon back down at the station. Davis remembered that he saw Edwards and the other thirty-six footer crew members still at the station when he returned from the tower, and the forty-footer had already left. Of course, that many years since this event, it is true that memories do fade. It is quite possible that the thirty-six footer left sometime after the forty-footer, perhaps as much as twenty to thirty minutes later. The tapes and notarized statements from all of the survivors of 12 January 1961 and January 1991, thirty years later, have been examined. There are some rather great differences between the statements taken in 1961 and in 1991; however, it is generally agreed that the statements given in 1961 are more accurate and usable.

Davis does remember that when he left the beacon room in the lighthouse, there was a strong wind blowing; and when he looked down at the bar, it appeared to be rough. Davis also stated that small craft warnings were up at the time. It is unknown why small craft warnings were displayed at the cape at 4:20 PM when at 2:00 PM, gale warnings were put up at the lightship eight miles away. Gale warnings meant that the anticipated winds would be around thirty-four to forty knots.

Normally, all stations in a given area were sent the same messages by the National Weather Service Marine on what warnings to display. It is possible that Davis had mistaken gale flags for small craft flags. Nevertheless, there seemed to be ample warning and signals of a weather change. At 2:00 PM, the lightship had been told by the weather service to hoist gale warnings. At 4:00 PM, the lightship reported to the weather service that winds were force 7, a gale at twenty-eight to thirty-three knots.

Ariel view of Cape Disappointments Boathouse 1961.
Boathouse was located about 1/3 of a mile from the station.

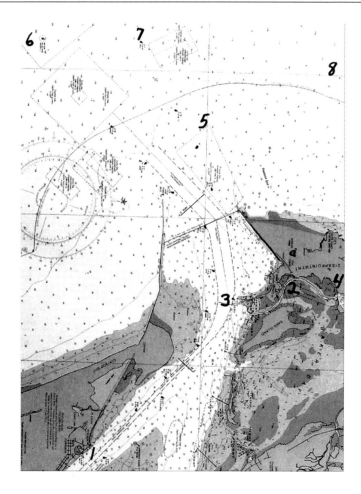

1. Pt. Adams, Hammond, Oregon
2. Cape Disappointment station, Ilwaco, Washington
3. Jana-Jo position at 3:30 PM when she called in for the Mermaid.
4. Ilwaco, Washington.
5. Mermaids approximant position at 3:30 PM
6. Columbia River Lightship.
7. Buoy number 1
8. Reported position that CG-40564 located the Mermaid and took her in tow.

12

Underway, on Scene, in Tow

After departing the boathouse and cranking up the *CG-40564* to full power, they headed out Baker Bay channel toward the Columbia River. BM1 Murray told everyone to get into their life jackets. Both he and Lowe put them on but did not secure the leg straps. Acie Maxwell put his on and included securing the leg straps. In the tower at Point Adams, SN Sussex had been monitoring the radio traffic in case it looked like the cape would need help from Point Adams. At around 4:30 PM, he heard the *CG-40564* radio the cape, telling them they had exited the Baker Bay channel and were heading outbound. He also heard them try to contact the *Mermaid* without receiving any reply.

Onboard the *CG-40564*, after entering the Columbia River, instead of taking a direct route outbound on the black buoy line that marked the right side of the channel, Murray turned 45 degrees to the right to cut across the middle ground. This route would take him through shallower waters outside the main channel over to the upper part of the north jetty area where, when well off the jetty, they would make a turn left to parallel the jetty. At times, this route might be preferred to avoid rough seas on the bar, but it also could offer many surprises in the way of large swells and sudden breaking seas.

Engineer Lowe was standing on the engine hatch behind the coxswain, holding on to the mast. Seaman Maxwell was standing on the coxswain platform by the radio, holding on to the handrails above the radio. Lowe has stated that they were running off the jetty with the lookout tower directly astern when something terrible happened. All of a sudden, the boat went up a huge swell and became airborne. Lowe said he was sure the boat had come completely out of the water. He, to this day, cannot figure out how what happened next came about. He was hanging on to the mast with a death grip when the boat came down hard almost knocking him to his knees.

When he looked up, he said he was looking directly over the windshield at the lookout tower. Somehow, the boat had performed a complete 180-degree turn to face the other way. The impact was so strong that the aluminum radio antenna broke in half. This should have been a very strong indication to Murray that this was no place for a forty-foot utility boat. This was not the case. When the boat had slammed down, Seaman Maxwell had hit his head on the radio set, making the outside radio inoperative and giving him a bleeding cut above his eyes. Murray told him to get the first aid kit and find a bandage of some type.

In short order, Murray straightened up the forty-footer and again was outbound at a high rate of speed. Larger swells were still coming at him, but he managed to quarter them (to put the boat's bow at an angle to the oncoming wave so that when she rode over the top, there would be a cushioning effect on the other side) and at times with speed reductions. When the boat passed by the end of the jetty, the crew could see that the Peacock Spit area had large breaking seas. It would seem, at around this time, that Murray would have checked for the whereabouts of the thirty-six footer or at least had the cape give Point Adams a heads-up call for the possible need of the *Triumph*. No records of any conversations between the thirty-six footer and a request for the *Triumph* have been found to be made at that time. It would seem that all resources should have been activated and made available as soon as Murray became aware of the actual conditions on the bar and at sea, but for unknown reasons, this was not done until some precious time had gone by.

Murray then headed for the vicinity of buoy 7, which was the last reported position of the *Mermaid*. Upon their arrival, they could find nothing.

Murray turned the helm over to Lowe so he could go inside to use the radio to try to contact the *Mermaid* on the commercial working frequency 2638. All Coast Guard boats, ships, and aircraft could communicate with all other vessels on all the civilian working frequencies. However, shore stations could not communicate with civilian vessels on their working frequencies. So that both vessels and shore units could communicate, they would have to do this on a compatible frequency such as 2182 or 2702. This was a continuing problem for many years and made it, at times, very difficult in emergencies to get accurate information. The radio was still operative inside the cabin and even with the broken antenna; they had communications with others within a few miles. When the outside speaker became inoperative, they tied the cabin door open with a piece of small line so as to be able to hear from the inside speaker. Murray soon received a response from the *Mermaid* on frequency 2638. He confirmed the *Mermaid*'s position as due west of North Head in thirty-one fathoms of water (ninety-six feet). He also got them to switch to frequency 2182, the national distress radio frequency. There was some discussion with the *Mermaid* to help Murray find them, and he asked them to flash their searchlight toward where the forty footer's location was.

All who had crewed on forty-footers with Murray have said that he was a great boat handler. On this day, his capabilities, and that of the boat and his crew, would be stretched to the limit and beyond. Murray did not seem to have any earlier experience operating the thirty-six-foot lifeboat in the surf. Before assignment at the cape, Murray had earlier been aboard a lightship off the northwest coast and had spent a tour at the Neah Bay Lifeboat Station.

Neah Bay was just inside the entrance to the Strait of Juan de Fuca and had thirty-six footers but did not have the surf and bar conditions that the coastal stations did. It is very important, if you are a coxswain at a lifeboat station, that you know the capabilities of the lifeboat. This is only acquired by actually taking the boat into the surf. EN2 Lowe stated that he did not recall ever going on surf drills in the thirty-six footer. It has always been Coast Guard policy that a lifeboat would not go into the surf without a backup lifeboat. The cape did not have such a backup boat at the time. It is also a possibility that if the cape wanted to have some surfboat drills, they would have to coordinate with Point Adams so that both stations could conduct training.

At around 4:45 PM, Sussex, in the Point Adams's tower, had been catching some of the attempts by the forty-footer on frequency 2182 to contact the *Mermaid*. It sounded as if conditions were deteriorating, and that there were problems in locating the *Mermaid*. Sussex picked up the phone, called the dayroom, and informed the officer of the day on what was going on with the cape. He did this to give a heads up for the possible need of the *Triumph* and the Point Adams's two other thirty-six-foot lifeboats.

Seaman Sussex and Seaman Ponton had become close friends while stationed at Point Adams. If a call came for the *Triumph*, Sussex wanted to be in on the action. He made a call to the dayroom and asked for Ponton.

When Ponton came on the line, Sussex asked him to take the tower watch so that he could go on the call. Ponton had been on the earlier run to the lightship and agreed to do this for Sussex if the coxswain said it was okay. Sussex sat back and waited for the call to come in for the need of the *Triumph*.

The competition between Point Adams and Cape Disappointment was very well-known. It would continue right up to 1967 when Point Adams closed, and both units were combined at Cape Disappointment. There was a continuous race to see who could accumulate the most cases in a given year. Sometimes one station would overhear the other working a case and divert a boat on patrol to intercept or make themselves a part of the case. This competition was good-natured and not dangerous to life or limb.

Around 5:00 PM, several things happened. Chief Porter arrived at the lookout tower and quickly assessed the situation. What he found was a very severe storm brewing and a breaking bar. He knew that anywhere out there was no place for his forty-foot utility boat. Porter picked up the radio, called the Point Adams tower, and told them that he needed the *Triumph* to get underway as soon as possible.

Seaman Sussex took the call at Point Adams, contacted the dayroom once again, and relayed this information to the officer of the day. He also talked to Doug Ponton and asked him to come up and relieve him.

Both Murray on the *CG-40564* and Chief Porter in the tower had been trying to get the *Mermaid* to come up on frequency 2182. The *Jana-Jo* radioed that she had the *Mermaid* switching over to frequency 2182. When the *Mermaid* was contacted, she was asked for her present position. The *Mermaid* stated that she was west of North Head Light in 31 fathoms (ninety-six feet) of water. The *CG-40564* had searched in that area a short time before and, evidently, had missed her due to weather conditions. Murray put the *CG-40564* on a course along the sixteen-fathom line and, at 5:15 PM, located the *Mermaid*. In later testimony, Terry Lowe stated that they were just outside the surf line west of North Head lighthouse and maybe north a little off Beards Hollow. Given the sea and weather conditions at the time, it seemed that the seas were breaking all around the area, and Lowe could have thought that they were just off the surf line. All during this time, the weather and seas were deteriorating.

The seas seemed to be running over twenty feet with wind-blown whitecaps on top. The wind was blowing at approximately forty knots with driving rain. Murray told Lowe and Maxwell that he would circle around, head into the seas, and approach the bow of the *Mermaid* to pass a towline. As soon as Murray had the boat on an approach, Lowe and Maxwell headed back to ready the towline. Lowe took a handful of nylon line from the reel and attached a small messenger heaving line to it. It was very dangerous on the back deck, and every place Lowe went, Maxwell had a hold of his belt and coat for safety purposes. Lowe had removed his life jacket because it was difficult to work in. Maxwell had his life jacket on with all straps attached while Murray had removed his and hung it over the railing behind him. Again, this was not policy and was very dangerous, but these bulky jackets made it very difficult for a coxswain to operate in extreme conditions.

It was also very dangerous for the Bergmans to come out on the bow of their boat to take a towline, but it had to be done. They both had their life jackets on that are of the same type that the Coast Guard used, but whether the leg straps were secured is not known.

Murray made a flawless approach, and when Lowe thought the time was right, he threw the heaving line that crossed the bow of the *Mermaid*. The Bergmans grabbed the line and pulled the towline across as Lowe and Maxwell let more out. It was very tricky in such rough conditions, and the possibility of getting the towline fouled in the screws or rudders was a very real one. If this happened, it could be fatal to all involved. Murray had both engines in gear while adjusting them for the power he needed to pass safely by the *Mermaid* and into the seas ahead. Lowe hollered that the towline was secure on the *Mermaid*. Murray told him to let as much line out as possible as he increased RPMs to gain some headway. Murray watched as the line went out, and when the *Mermaid* was about six hundred feet behind, he yelled at Lowe to make it fast on the tow bit. When this was done, Lowe and Maxwell ran up behind the cabin where they could get some protection. Conditions were just terrible, and Murray knew they were operating on the edge of survival. Worse was to come.

As Murray headed the *CG-40564* into the seas and the storm, the boat went over the top of one wave and down the backside; the *Mermaid* would disappear from view. He had Lowe take the wheel while he went inside to contact the cape and give a situation report. When he called, Chief Porter came back to him. Murray told him that they had taken the *Mermaid* in tow and were heading in a southerly direction but were making very slow progress. Chief Porter told him that he had requested the *Triumph* to come out to assist them, and if she were not underway yet, she would be shortly.

Porter directed Murray to proceed to the vicinity of buoy 1 and await the arrival of the *Triumph*.

At the time, no one really realized the conditions on the bar and the surrounding area. Under the right conditions, the bar has been known to break all the way across and out past buoy 1. Heading north to south toward the lightship across the mouth of the river during these conditions could prove disastrous. It would have seemed prudent to stay as far away from the mouth of the river as possible even if that meant trying to head offshore. One possibility was to let the storm push them north toward Grays Harbor. Even though the seas and weather were bad and not looking like there was going to let up, the *CG-40564* and *Mermaid* would ride it out for the next couple of hours. On the *CG-40564*, everyone was wet and cold to the core. There was no place to dry out and get warm. The wind was blowing the rain so hard that when it would hit exposed skin, it was like needles hitting them. The only comfort the crew had was knowing that the *Triumph* was on her way out. Since they took the *Mermaid* in tow, they had not heard or seen the lifeboat *CG-36454*. By this time, Murray figured she should be in the area.

13

Motor Lifeboat *Triumph* Underway

The Point Adams crew had been monitoring the radio in the station's office, and Ponton told Sussex that BM1 Culp had picked Ponton to go on the call. Sussex asked him to talk to Culp and see if Sussex could go in Ponton's place. Ponton told Sussex the weather was really picking up, and it was going to be nasty out there.

"You know how you get seasick," Ponton said.

Sussex replied, "Yes, I know."

But he thought that this might be the time he could lick the problem. Ponton said that he would ask Culp and let him know. Soon, Sussex heard the pounding of someone coming up the ladder, and then the trap door to below opened and up popped Ponton's head.

He told Sussex that Culp had said it would be okay, but he had to get down as soon as he could. Sussex gave Ponton a quick rundown on what was going on and headed below to his room to get his foul-weather jacket. Sussex desperately wanted to get over his seasick problem. It had been a continuing one of which, if it remained, could be a deciding factor as to whether he would remain at a lifeboat station or, for that matter, in the Coast Guard for a career.

BM1 Miller was the officer of the day at Point Adams. A short time before the call came in, his wife, Joan, called and asked if he could come home for a few minutes so she could run an errand. BM1 Culp was still at the station and was in the day room playing cribbage with one of the other crew. Miller asked him if he would take over his duties for a few minutes while he went home. Culp told him that was not a problem and to go on home. The Millers lived less then half a block from the Coast Guard station. Shortly after Miller left, the first call from Sussex in the tower came, informing them about what was going on with the cape's case. Culp quickly moved the cribbage game into the station's office where he could monitor the radio.

When the call came in for the *Triumph*, Culp had been contemplating whom he would take with him. Even though he did not have the duty that night, he was standing in for Miller at the time and had every intention of going. The crews at lifeboat stations lived for the calls that would come in. He could have called up Miller and asked him to come back and take the call, but he was caught up in the excitement.

Culp quickly picked BM2 John Hoban to come along as well as Seaman Boatswains Mate Ralph Mace, Engineman Third Class Joseph Petrin, and Engineman Third Class Gordon Huggins. Culp had picked Seaman Ponton but agreed to take Seaman Sussex in his place. Sussex's problem with seasickness was known to Culp, yet he respected Sussex's efforts in trying to get over it. Culp had plenty of backup men in case Sussex would become so sick he could not perform his job. Maybe in hindsight, he should have taken Ponton, but he was not aware of how terrible the conditions would soon become.

Just as Culp and the men were heading out, Junior Meyer walked into the office, and Culp spotted him. He shouted, "Hey, June, you want to come along for old time sake?" Junior politely declined, stating that he had to catch the ferry to the Washington side soon and wished everyone good luck. All the men Culp picked had a vast knowledge of their jobs onboard lifeboats and were all seasoned team players.

At this point, the case was nothing but routine. Culp instructed the men at the station to contact Chief Berto and BM1 Miller and bring them up to date on who would be going on the *Triumph* with him. Everyone loaded the station vehicles and headed for the Hammond mooring basin. They had to travel through the small town for about one-half mile to get to the boat, and they moved as quickly as possible. All records state that the call came in at 5:00 PM, and that the *Triumph* departed at 5:05 PM. Considering the distance to travel and the time to get the boat operational and lines off, it would seem more probable that it was a short time later than 5:05 PM.

Seaman Ponton, in the point's tower, could barely make out the running lights of the *Triumph* as she left the dock and headed toward the harbor entrance. It was a short time before a voice on the radio, that sounded like SNBM Mace, advised the point that that the *Triumph* was underway. Ponton acknowledged the call and told him to have a good trip.

The *Triumph* entered the river, and Culp pointed the bow toward the lighthouse at the cape, which was barely visible. He instructed everyone to get into their life jackets, and all complied. Throughout the Coast Guard, the men knew that to be able to get the job done, they would have to get out of the life jackets at times. Those who have put on one of those old bulky life jackets know how cumbersome they could be and how restrictive they made a person feel who was trying to do a necessary job.

The tide had been on the flood for a couple of hours and was pushing upriver at close to one knot. This, combined with the slow flat-out speed of the *Triumph* of around nine knots, put the outbound speed of the boat at eight knots. As they went past Fort Stevens light to the south, they began to feel the wind-driven rain hitting their faces. Culp contacted the cape's tower to get a position of the *CG-40564* and the *Mermaid*. Chief Porter told him that the forty-footer had the *Mermaid* in tow and was making slow headway toward buoy one. Chief Porter also informed Culp that the wind was blowing hard out of the south and gusting up to forty knots. There also were severe rainsqualls going through the area, and that the bar area was not visible from the cape. Culp was also told that the *CG-36454* was out there somewhere and was asked to keep an eye out for them. Culp acknowledged this information and told Chief Porter that it would be an hour or more to get out to buoy 1 and longer if he encountered a breaking bar.

As the *Triumph* approached buoy 12, those onboard could start to feel the large swells running beneath the boat. It was getting dark outside now, and along with the weather conditions, visibility was very poor. Culp reduced power to around five knots as he strained to make out any signs of the conditions ahead.

He instructed everyone to let him know if they saw anything. BM2 Hoban hollered out, "Running lights dead ahead." Culp saw them then and, immediately, gave full right rudder so as to safely pass portside to portside. The running lights were those of the pilot boat, *Peacock*. Culp picked up the radio transmitter and called the *Peacock*, asking what the conditions were on the bar.

The operator came back and stated that they did not encounter any breakers on the way in, but there were some large swells. Visibility was very poor so they could not tell Culp what the conditions were elsewhere on the bar other than down the red buoy line. Buoy 12 was just on the inside of the bar, but this area of the buoy, at times, was known to break upriver. Culp must have started feeling a little apprehensive about what was ahead of him. He had made several rough crossings of the bar, but never on a breaking bar at night. Very few men, back then and to this day, have crossed a breaking bar at night. It has been done but is very dangerous. Coxswains just cannot see the breakers coming, and the darkness makes it almost impossible to judge the wave as to height or if it is about to break.

Culp had confidence in his crew and boat. His destination was the vicinity of buoy 1 to meet up with the *CG-40564* and assist them with the tow. This meant that he had to travel along the black buoy line. He could not help but get the feeling that this was not going to go good. He eased the *Triumph* to a slow speed toward the black line and the right side of the channel. As he did so, the *Triumph* along with her pitching started its lumbering roll. This triggered a reaction from Seaman Sussex, and he immediately lost his dinner over the side. Before things got worse, Hoban told Sussex to go forward and lie down in one of the bow berths. Sussex felt terrible about this, but he knew he was out of commission as far as assisting his shipmates, if needed. He knew that they would soon have enough to put up without worrying about him.

Huggins was standing on deck by the forward cabin with the rest of the men when he felt his nose running. At first, that is what he thought it was—just a runny nose. He then tasted blood in his mouth and went into the cabin to get some light and see what was happening. This was when he found out that he had a bloody nose. He could not understand how this happened as he had not hit his nose or head on anything. He grabbed some tissue and stuffed it up his nose, but this failed to stop the blood flow. He told Culp what was going on, and Culp told him to lay down on a forward berth to see if that would help. Sussex, by this time, was feeling really miserable and getting sick up forward, so Huggins told Culp he would go to the aft compartment and try to lay down there.

Culp agreed to this and, at the same time, thinking he had just started out; and he was already two men down. He knew that with the remainder of the men, he could still accomplish the mission if nothing else serious happened. He hated to shut the door with Sussex in there, but they needed to seal up the boat as best possible for the conditions they would be going into.

Culp contacted the *CG-40564* and asked for an update of their position. Lowe came back and said that they were somewhere in the area of buoys 3 and 1 but did not know their exact position. He said they were bow into the seas with the *Mermaid* trailing behind. One thing that no one seemed to realize was the fact that, in combination with the flood tide and storm out of the south, all the boats involved would be pushed shoreward and to the north. The tidal current at the time was going toward the northeast, and with the weather, conditions could prove to be a deadly combination. Everything operating in the area would be pushed into the area where sea conditions were steadily getting worse. They would be shoved into Peacock Spit and to the vicinity of what could be another deadly obstacle—the unlighted can buoy 5. None of the boats had radar, and in the stormy dark conditions, the only way to spot buoy 5 was with a searchlight that could pick up the reflective tape that was on it. The can buoys at both the Columbia and Grays Harbor bars were placed there because during storms, the seas would constantly break over them.

A lighted buoy was much higher in structure and offered more area for the seas to push on. This could result in the buoy breaking loose of its moorings and drifting off. Even in calm seas at night, the prudent mariner gave these can buoys a wide berth. It would be several years before the Coast Guard came up with a suitable lighted buoy to replace those unlighted can buoys.

Keeping all the above in mind, Culp steered the *Triumph* on a course outbound but well inside the black line. Every once in awhile, he could see a light from a buoy. Being that visibility was so bad, he felt that this light was coming from buoy 9, which was just inside of the end of the north jetty. The light was not visible all the time at its rated sequence. This gave Culp the indication that there must be some large seas running in the area. The sea would pass under the buoy and, when it passed by, would drop the buoy into the trough behind it where it would remain out of sight for a longer period.

Cape Disappointments CG-36454, 1960.

MLB Triumph at Pt. Adams dock in configuration she was 12 January 1961.

14

Crossing the Bar Outbound

As long as he could see a buoy light or some other aids-to-navigation, Culp could pretty well judge his position. At the time, he would have to buoy hop and go from one visible light to the next one if he could pick it up. He looked over to his right and could just make out the range light and lighthouse at Cape Disappointment. While approaching the bar area, the *Triumph* received a call from Point Adams directing them to proceed to the vicinity of the Columbia River Lightship and await better conditions after taking over the tow.

As Culp left the buoy light ahead well off his starboard bow and headed outbound, he felt the bow of the *Triumph* pitch up sharply. He yelled for everyone to hang on and throttled up the engine. The swell moved under them, and just as the bow came clear, the swell broke beneath the keel. With the momentum of the boat, they found themselves charging through the wave to the other side with the bow pitching almost straight down. When the bow dug into the bottom of the trough, everyone on deck was pressed against the wheelhouse. The boat recovered from this, and Culp throttled down and prepared to meet the next one that he knew must be coming. Luckily, no one was seriously injured. This would prove to be one of the worst bar crossings any of them had ever experienced, and the irony of all this was that when they arrived on the scene, they would still be on the bar. Sometimes Culp could not make much headway at all, and the progress was very slow. Taking a beating as they were, it would be some time to finally get to the *CG-40564* and the *Mermaid*.

BM1 Larry Geer and other crew members at Westport had been monitoring the radio at their station since the case down south had started. As explained earlier, this station was where the MLB *Invincible*, the sister boat to the *Triumph*, had been attached. However, the *Invincible* was sent to Coos Bay, Oregon, a month earlier with the arrival of the new steel

MLB, *CG-52313*. Geer and the other men felt great empathy for their shipmates down south. They would have tried to help if called upon, but they were over forty miles away, and with the weather and sea conditions off Grays Harbor, it would take them many hours to beat their way there. Even if they would have tried, they might have not been able to make any headway south.

The towing lines on all the boats attached to station Cape Disappointment on 12 January 1961, had been changed from manila to three-strand nylon. This was a much superior product than the old manila lines that had been in use. The manila lines were prone to rot, and they were checked constantly. There also was no give or stretch to the manila lines. The nylon lines were rot resistant and had the ability to stretch over 15 percent of their length before parting. This characteristic was one that was wanted in a line while towing in rough waters. The thirty-six-foot lifeboats and the *Triumph* at Point Adams had not been changed over to the nylon line and were still using the old manila lines for towing. It was the same old story—money. A directive had come down to convert all towlines as needed when unit money allowed it.

Around 6:30 PM, the Astoria-Megler Ferry departed. Junior and Evelyn Meyer had just made it to the ferry in time. After he had parked his car, they went up one deck to the passenger lounge. The ferry captains are licensed by the Coast Guard and were widely experienced. Meyer took note of the weather outside. It was raining hard, visibility was low, and it seemed to be blowing a gale against the portside of the ferry. They took a seat for the half-hour crossing. When the ferry arrived on the Washington side, the captain had great difficulty in docking.

He made several attempts but kept bouncing off the pilings. The weather was making the maneuvers required difficult, but finally the captain got the ferry bow into the dock and held it there with the engines. They hurried down to their car as they wanted off as soon as they were allowed. After leaving the ferry, they headed down the two-lane highway leading to Ilwaco, Washington. On the way, the road ran parallel to the Columbia River; and in places, the storm was blowing water and debris onto the road. Meyer strained to see ahead all the way to Ilwaco where he took the road marked North Head. They arrived at the light station and met BM1 Webb just as he was leaving. It was not that Meyer had never met BM1 Webb before as he had been on many calls with Webb when they had been stationed together at Point Adams. Webb told Meyer what was going on and for him to come down to the cape's station as soon as he could. Evelyn and the kids would stay in their new quarters until Meyer returned.

Webb had been informed of what was happening when Chief Porter called him and asked him to come up to the tower and help out. Engineer Third Class Grover Dillard was an engineer from Cape Disappointment that lived in government housing at North Head. Together, Meyer and Dillard drove down to the station and asked what they could do. As a precautionary measure, they were directed by Chief Porter from the tower to take a four-wheel drive vehicle with radio and go to the Benson Beach area and standby.

After driving up to cape's lookout tower, BM1 Webb walked the short distance to the tower almost bending over at a 45-degree angle against pelting rain and very strong winds. Before entering the tower, he looked out toward where the end of the north jetty would be and saw absolutely no sign of light from buoys or boats. When he entered the tower, Chief Porter greeted him and told him thanks for coming over as he needed some moral support. Porter knew Webb very well from Webb's years of experience at Point Adams and knew he could count on him for advice or anything else that might come up. Webb noted that after his entrance to the tower, there seemed to be very little, if any, chatter on the radio or from Chief Porter. Webb could tell that Chief Porter was very bothered by what was going on, and he knew from what little he had heard of the situation that this was something that could turn very ugly in a short time. Chief Porter told Webb that he had just directed Dillard and Meyer to go to Benson Beach and standby for further instructions.

Webb took the chance and asked the chief if he was okay. Porter answered him by saying, "No, I am not. I have two of my boats and my men out in this crap with one boat that certainly should not be there and the other the *CG-36454* with some good, but not very experienced men aboard." He had earlier asked for the *Triumph* from Point Adams. He told Webb that she was somewhere below, attempting to cross the bar, and he was worried for them as well as the others. "Yes, John, I am worried about this one." John could understand how the chief felt and told him he was there to do whatever was necessary to help him out.

About the same time the ferry had left Astoria, the pilot boat, *Peacock*, tied up to the Point Adams boathouse dock for a crew change. Soon after, Jim Messer, a mate on the *Peacock*, came aboard; he relieved for the 7:00 PM-1:00 AM watch. Messer asked about the weather conditions and was informed that the weather was not too bad—a little choppy and disagreeable. He was also told that Coast Guard boats were on the bar assisting the crab boat *Mermaid*. From all other conditions reported on the bar from 6:00 to 8:00 PM, they were not as mild as the one Messer had received. Perhaps it was because, while inbound and in the dark and having the seas on the stern or stern quarter, they had a smoother ride. When the *Triumph* started across the bar at 6:00 PM, there were reported twenty- to thirty-foot breaking seas at their position.

Shortly after the *Triumph* had departed for the bar, BM1 Miller arrived back at the station. He went into the station's office and picked up the radio to call Culp to see how things were going. Culp told him that he would be coming up on the bar in about thirty minutes, but judging from the strong winds and driving rains, it might be a rough crossing. Miller told him that, just in case, he was going to get ready boat crews for the two lifeboats left at Point Adams. Miller knew that he would be the coxswain on the *CG-36535*, and he quickly picked the engineer, Engineer Third Class Larry Fredrickson. He picked up the phone and called the tower telling Seaman Ponton that if needed, Ponton was to go on the *CG-36535*. Miller told him that if this happened, Ponton was to leave the tower, get his gear, and prepare to leave. Someone in the office would assume the radio watch.

BM1 Hernando Lopez was still onboard, and Miller called him into the office. Lopez was one of the newer boatswain mates at the lifeboat station, coming from many years on larger Coast Guard ships. Miller knew that Lopez had been out on quite a few calls since his arrival and was being trained by other coxswains, but never on a heavy weather call. Miller had an idea and put it to Lopez. He asked him how he felt about taking a crew and the *CG-36554* over to the Cape Disappointment station.

The reason Miller told him about going to the cape was because he was thinking about BM1 Webb at North Head Light. He told Lopez that if needed, he wanted Lopez to take the *CG-36554* over to the cape's boathouse and pick up Webb. Lopez said that doing this would not be a problem, and that in fact he welcomed it because he knew of his limited experience and of Webb and his qualifications as a boat coxswain. For the engineer on the *CG-36554*, Miller picked a highly qualified man, Engineer Second Class Larry Dixon, and for the seaman, Ronnie Jansson who was also being trained. About the time Miller had set the boat crews, Senior Chief Berto returned to the station. Miller quickly filled him in on what was going on up to now and of the preparations he had made. Berto told him that he agreed and took a chair to listen in on any radio conversations from the boats.

The officer in charge of lifeboat stations placed great trust in the men they oversaw. They were very well assessed on the abilities of each man. When the coxswains were out on the boats, the decisions were all theirs, and the chief would normally just give advice if he thought it was needed. With the abilities of BM1 Miller, Berto had the utmost confidence in him. Miller had been at the station for a few years and had a vast knowledge of the boats and the area. In fact, Miller would be up for promotion to chief; and Berto believed that, once promoted, he would soon be in charge of his own station. As for Miller's decision to send the *CG-36554* over to pick up Webb, Berto totally agreed. BM1 Webb had, until a short time before, been stationed at Point Adams for six years, rising in rank from seaman apprentice to first class boatswains mate. Webb also had been raised locally and had vast knowledge of the area, boats, and bar and was a fully qualified surfman. Hopefully, none of these preparations would be needed, but just in case, they would be ready.

On the bar and ahead of the *Triumph* around this time was the lifeboat *CG-36454* from Cape Disappointment with coxswain Seaman Boatswains Mate Larry Edwards and his crew. They had departed from the boathouse some time after the *CG-40564*, and Edwards's crew consisted of Engineer Fireman Brian Johnson and Seaman Apprentice Jim Croker.

As Edwards brought the lifeboat around jetty A and into the river heading outbound, the full force of the wind and rain hit them head on. It was starting to get dark out, and along with the storm, it made for limited visibility. Edwards noticed large swells coming by their present position, and they had not yet passed buoy 11 at the entrance to Baker Bay. He had been across the bar many times both in daylight and in the dark. Most of those crossings had been in decent weather conditions. He had never been across a breaking bar at night. Edwards told everyone to tighten up on all their life-jacket straps and prepare for what might be a very rough ride. Edwards throttled down to half speed (about five knots) and pointed the bow of the lifeboat straight out the channel and inside the black buoy line.

It was not long before the *CG-36454* started to encounter very rough conditions with larger breaking swells. Edwards started to see white water all around him, indicating swells that had already crested and broken.

When he felt the bow of the boat rise, he would increase power getting through before the break, and at other times, a swell would break onto the bow of the lifeboat.

Edwards was listening in on the radio as they proceeded out. He could hear the *CG-40564* on the radio and heard the *Triumph* talking to Point Adams. This did give them some comfort in knowing that they were not alone out there. As for the radio onboard the *CG-36454*, the only transmitter was on the starboard side of the coxswain's platform inside a latched watertight compartment. The speaker was watertight and on the outside. When in heavy weather or taking seas from astern and with the radio box open to the elements, it could be disabled by the water. When they had left the boathouse, they had called the cape's tower with an underway message. As stated before, the exact time of the *CG-36454*'s departure is not known. No radio logs are available, and assistance reports stated both the *CG-40564* and the *CG-36454* left at 4:20 PM. Edwards chose to not make any unnecessary transmissions until he got across the bar in what he hoped would be calmer waters. He had overheard the tower tell the *CG-40564* to head for the vicinity of buoy 1 with their tow, so this would be the position Edwards would set as his course.

At around 6:00 PM and after crossing a very rough bar, Edwards was just east of buoy 1. He had to be watchful because sea conditions were confused, and large swells were still passing beneath the *CG-36454*. For a young boatswain mate and his crew, this so far had been a scary learning experience.

Edwards had pushed the limits of his boat while crossing out. Because he could not tell when a swell might break, he had powered full throttle up them. This meant, at times, the boat would fly off the top and land with tremendous force in the trough at the back of the swell. That these boats could survive this type of abuse is testimony to their ruggedness. The alternative to not breaking through the swell would be the possibility of the breaker throwing the boat backward, pitch poling (end over end) the boat and maybe losing the crew overboard. As Edwards and his crew looked around, the only light they could see was the one flashing from buoy 1. Edwards elected to stem the seas and stay as close to his present position as possible. He then took the chance to open the radio box and sent a position report to the cape. When he called in, Chief Porter told him to stay where he was, and that the *CG-40564* was slowly making it toward him. Edwards told Chief Porter of their rough bar crossing, and that conditions where they were at the present were just about as bad.

Back on the bar, the *Triumph* was having extreme difficulties. All that Culp could do was head directly into whatever might be ahead of him. His visibility had become even more limited. Being that it was dark and so stormy out, he did not have the benefit of finding a calmer area of the bar. If he had radar, at least he could get some feedback from sea return on the radar screen. This way, he would have some kind of an idea of where the roughest part of the bar might be. Culp had to navigate within these restricted waters with a compass and a fathometer and the eyes and ears of his crew.

The *Triumph* had heard the call from the *CG-40564* and from Edwards on the *CG-36454*. All the *Triumph* crew could do was hang on and let Culp do his best at guiding the *Triumph* through these terrible seas. He was committed to taking the *Triumph* through this and could not turn around. If he attempted to turn around, he would risk taking a breaker broadside, which could prove disastrous to them. So far, this ride had been just gut-wrenching. If there were somewhere on the *Triumph* where one would get a decent ride, that would be in the aft compartment where Huggins was. The worst place to be would be up forward where Seaman Sussex was. Culp could do nothing for Sussex until they got into some calmer waters. Then, if things were right, maybe he could get Sussex to the after compartment.

15

Changing of the Tow

On the *Triumph*, the radio operation was the same with Edwards on the *CG-36454*. They did not want to open the watertight box to transmit for fear of disabling the outside unit. The *Triumph* did have an inside pilothouse handset, but getting to this meant opening the door, which they did not want to do. Aboard the *Mermaid*, the Bergman brothers were becoming increasingly concerned with their predicament. They had, when the *CG-40564* took them in tow, strung a bucket off the stern so that the *Mermaid* would follow along without veering off one way or another. It had been a very confused sea when the *CG-40564* had finally located them and took them in tow.

They must have felt, at the time, some relief from the Coast Guard's arrival; but the concern was that they were being towed toward the bar, and the sea conditions were getting worse. It seemed that they were being towed from the frying pan into the fire. The Bergmans had been monitoring their radio and had overheard the Coast Guard talking back and forth about their plans. They did not think much about the idea of the Coast Guard towing them in or cutting across the middle ground to the lightship. They might not have had as much experience as some of the other fishermen in the area, but they were very savvy about the local area and the treacherous bar. They also knew that their boat was far more superior to riding out rough seas than the Coast Guard boat that had them in tow up to now. They hoped that when the *Triumph* arrived and took them in tow, they could talk them into going out to sea away from this very dangerous area.

It was around 7:15 PM when the *Triumph* had sighted the *CG-40564* and the *Mermaid* in what Culp must have felt were very dangerous seas. Culp's instinct about the sea conditions in the area would shortly be noted in his conversation with the *CG-40564*. There are many discrepancies in the various testimonies and records as far as the time for where the various units and boats may have been during the search and towing sequence, perhaps as much as thirty minutes or more. This might have been attributed to things happening so fast that time and other pertinent items were entered after the fact. The times of future happenings in a short period, if put down on a nautical chart, would show movement of all boats being closer to the area of buoy 3 than 1 upon the arrival of the *Triumph*.

By 7:15 PM or so, the tide had been on the flood for about three hours and was moving in at around 1.9 knots. This, in combination with the huge seas and the wind from a southerly direction, would be pushing the boats that were trying to hold their position inbound at two to three knots. They were all being pushed inbound and toward Peacock Spit in a northeasterly direction. Culp knew that whatever decision was to be made, it had to be made as soon as possible. When he observed the situation of the forty-footer, he—at first—thought that it might be better to have the forty-footer continue the tow out to sea with the *Triumph* following along. Even though he knew that the *CG-40564* should not be out there, things at the time were fairly stable with the tow. Chief Berto knew that any final decisions as to where Culp should tow the *Mermaid* would be up to Culp. Berto did pass on to him that if he thought he could manage it to tow the *Mermaid* out toward the lightship.

Onboard the *CG-40564*, Lowe had been talking to the *Triumph* and wanted to know when they were going to take over the tow. Culp came back to him stating that conditions were too rough where they were and to stand by. Lowe then called the cape and told Chief Porter that the *Triumph* was refusing to take the tow.

Onboard the *Triumph*, Culp had overheard this conversation; and he felt that, against his better judgment, he should take the tow. He directed his crew on deck to make ready the towline. EN3 Petrin went aft to the doghouse and, when he thought it was okay, opened the door. He yelled below to Huggins to pass up a heaving line, which Huggins did. Huggins asked Petrin if they needed his help, and Petrin responded that no, they had everything under control.

On deck, SNBM Mace and BM2 Hoban made ready to tow by taking down the after lifelines and making the four-inch manila towline ready. The four-inch towline was located on a large reel that was attached to the side of the aft doghouse just forward of the tow bit. Every move they made on the aft deck area had to be done with the utmost care. They had to move from one handhold to the other of which there were few and, at times, hang on to the one who had the most secure grip on something. There was the very real danger of being washed overboard at any time. It was very cumbersome for Mace and Hoban to work with the towline, but they managed to get a small amount off the reel and over the tow bit so that Petrin could tie the smaller messenger line to the eye. Petrin quickly did this and yelled to Culp that they were ready to pass the towline. Culp had then called the forty-footer and told them to drop the tow.

On the forty-footer, Lowe had picked up Culp's call, acknowledged it, and headed outside to help Maxwell pull in their towline. Lowe has stated that he never saw any other boat up to this time other than the *Mermaid*. When Lowe got back to where Maxwell was on the aft deck of the boat, he assisted him in pulling in and stowing the line. He could hear the engines revving up and feel the propellers turning as Murray maneuvered the forty-footer away. After Murray was well clear of the *Triumph* and the *Mermaid*, he had called for Lowe and Maxwell to come forward to where he stood on the coxswain's platform behind what little protection they could get from the wheelhouse.

16

Disaster

In what seems to be one of the most bewildering decisions that Murray had made so far, he drew Lowe and Maxwell to him. He said that he wanted a vote from them on whether they wanted to head in or try to make it to the lightship. The men had been out in those very hazardous conditions for several hours and, on top of that, were wet and cold to the core. Murray should have known from observing the conditions where he was now and from the reports of conditions further in from the *Triumph* what would be the best thing to do. For some reason, Lowe and Maxwell said that they wanted to try to head in, and Murray agreed. On the board of investigation conducted later, it was said that Murray was going to attempt to, under escort of *CG-36454*, proceed slowly toward the bar. However, they were on the bar. Murray wanted to ascertain if a bar crossing was possible as sea conditions were making it necessary for the *CG-40564* to seek shelter.

You cannot sneak up on the back of a bar such as the one at the Columbia River at night in twenty-to thirty-foot seas and sixty knot winds and expect anything but a catastrophe. In future investigations and interviews, Murray talked often about the middle ground of the bar area between buoys 1and 2 as being similar to the cabbage patch outside of San Francisco Bay. This area is full of sandbars and other shallow areas that one would want to avoid during storms. He was right in it being similar, but the mouth of the Columbia could become much worse. With this knowledge, Murray should have had only one choice to possibly save his boat and crew. That choice should have been to head, as closely as possible, in a northwesterly direction offshore as far away from the bar as he could get. Once farther offshore, the boat's bow could have been put into the seas, and they could have ridden out the storm the rest of the night. At least, the next morning, with some light, they could approach the bar and see what the conditions might have been by then. The *CG-36454* should then have been directed to stay with the *Triumph* as a standby boat. Neither of these decisions were made, and Murray proceeded inbound. Murray instructed Lowe to go inside the cabin, give the cape's tower a call, and let them know what the plan was.

When Lowe entered the cabin and called the cape, Chief Porter immediately picked up the transmitter and answered him. Lowe told him that they were proceeding inbound with the *CG-36454* tagging along. Chief Porter and BM1 Webb were horrified when they heard this. Porter called back to tell them to not attempt returning over the bar and heard nothing but silence in return. He then called for the *CG-36454*, and it was the same. Silence.

Off to one side of the forty-footer, Edwards and the *CG-36454* had been listening to the conversation from Murray and the tower. As he and his crew had shortly before come out across a very rough bar, he could not understand Murray's decision to try to head in. Edwards was really in no hurry to venture back into some of the worst seas he had ever encountered in his short career. However, he was a junior boatswains mate and would follow orders. He knew that this would be no easy task. There is not much you can do when you cannot see what might be coming. Also, a large swell could build up behind and, all of a sudden, break right over the boat. When this happens and the boat is underway, it might be picked up and thrown forward. The crew could be ripped loose, thrown overboard, or severely injured. There also could be severe damage done to the boat. Edwards put the *CG-36454* in gear and headed inbound as he observed the *CG-40564* disappear in the darkness ahead.

Onboard the *Triumph*, Culp was lining up to pass close to the bow of the *Mermaid* as safely as he could. He yelled over the noise to Mace to go inside the cabin, contact the *Mermaid*, and tell them to standby to receive the towline and make it fast to their bow cleat. It was all Culp could do to maneuver the *Triumph* forward into the large swells. He again yelled over his shoulder to Petrin and Hoban to go ahead and send the line across when they felt it was the right time. This way, Culp could give his full attention to operating the boat. As he crossed the bow of the *Mermaid*, he could see one of the Bergmans on the bow. Very shortly, Petrin hollered "line across!" followed by "towline secure on the *Mermaid*." Culp maintained his slow forward momentum as the towline was let out. Below in the aft cabin, Huggins stated that he could hear the noise the tow reel was making as the line went out. As he lay there, he heard a loud bang, followed by a lot of engine and propeller noise as the *Triumph* seemed to be maneuvering.

On deck, Hoban and Petrin had made the towline secure as directed by Culp and went forward to get some protection from the cabin. Culp slowly added some power to get some headway and get out of this area. As soon as he got some momentum forward, he felt the bow of the *Triumph* rise sharply as they climbed up a large swell and slid down the back of it. This happened so fast Culp did not have a chance to back off the throttle.

When the *Triumph* settled into the trough on the backside of the wave, Culp looked behind him and could see no sign of the *Mermaid* on the other side of the swell. As he looked, he observed the towline passing under the wave and still seemingly hooked to the *Mermaid*. Then, with a noise that sounded like a shotgun discharge, the line parted somewhere. Just as the towline had been connected, Mace came out of the cabin, shut the door, and was standing next to Culp. When the towline parted, Culp told Hoban and Petrin to go aft and pull in the remainder of the towline, and he would maneuver to make another pass at the *Mermaid*. He told Mace to go back inside, contact the *Mermaid* and the station, and let them know what they were doing. Mace did this and was overheard by the *Mermaid* and both stations. When Point Adams and the cape came back to Mace to acknowledge his transmission, all they got was silence.

On the deck of the *Triumph*, as Culp maneuvered to make another pass at the *Mermaid*, he had to bring the *Triumph* broadside to the swell, continue his turn, head past the *Mermaid*, and turn around again. It was while he was in the middle of the turn and broadside that a huge swell came along and broke directly over the *Triumph*. When this happened, it cleared the deck of all personnel and rolled the *Triumph* over to an upside-down position where she remained.

Aboard the pilot boat, *Peacock*, Messer guided her outbound toward the bar, and as he was doing so, he was hearing conversations between the *Triumph* and *Mermaid*. Most of these conversations were about concerns with towlines and rough sea conditions. As the *Peacock* proceeded downriver and neared the bar area, the winds seemed to be increasing and moving somewhat to the southwest. When the *Peacock* was rounding buoy 8 and lining up on the main outbound range toward the lightship, they experienced their first heavy swell. Messer knew then that the bar was more than "just a little choppy and disagreeable."

Continuing toward buoy 6, Messer reduced RPMs to slow down, and it was shortly that they began encountering large swells with some occasional breaks.

The wind and seas were steadily increasing. The bar area between buoys 6 and 5 was another area called the middle ground. Looking into the darkness in that direction, Messer saw a lot of white water indicating breaking seas. When he checked the radar picture, he saw a large quantity of sea return also indicating breaking seas. It was with great difficulty that the *Peacock* arrived off buoy 4 and entered the middle of a large squall. Seas were very rough, visibility was poor, and winds were gusting forty to fifty knots. Messer had been listening to the conversation between the *Mermaid* and *Triumph* for some time. He knew they were having difficulty, and that the towline had parted once. Consideration was being given by the *Peacock* to try to give some aid by traveling out to sea and around the middle ground area. They would then come inbound along the black buoy line. There was a great possibility that by following this plan in an attempt to help the *Mermaid* and the *Triumph*, their own lives and the *Peacock* might end up in a disastrous and losing situation.

Onboard the *CG-40564*, Lowe had just gotten through with his message to the cape when there was a very sharp rise of the boat's stern; one that pressed him securely against the inside cabin bulkhead. He could hear what sounded like the engines screaming at full power. In just a second or two, the forty-footer was flipped stern over onto its top. The interior cabin instantly filled with water, and Lowe found himself submerged and groping around, trying to find something familiar so he could get out. He had remembered from earlier training to become familiar with where all the inside equipment was located, and what he remembered would save his life now. In an upside-down configuration under water and in the dark, it can be most confusing. As he felt around, he grabbed hold of something and recognized it as the salvage pump that was bolted to the inside deck. He knew the pump was located just inside the cabin door. Working as quickly as possible, he further felt around and found the cabin door. He pulled himself through to the top of the boat's main deck just above him. He needed to find the port lifeline, get himself over or through, and go to the surface.

Just when he felt he could no longer hold his breath, he had miraculously made it out to the surface and was alongside the overturned boat. If he had put his life jacket on as required, it was quite possible that he would not have made it out of the capsized boat.

When the forty-footer went over, Maxwell was thrown clear. Murray was trapped under and in the well deck area. Murray stated that he grabbed his life jacket as the forty-footer went over and slipped into it. This was a physical impossibility. Murray's jacket had been hanging over the rail that was across the back of the coxswain's platform. Not having the life jacket on most likely saved Murray's life by allowing him to work his way out from beneath the boat. Murray surfaced behind the forty-footer and found the balsa life raft floating next to him. He grabbed hold of the lifelines attached to it and hung on as tightly as he could. As Lowe floated next to the capsized boat, he heard someone yelling. The voice seemed to be coming from the top of the capsized hull. He yelled back and heard the voice say, "Over here." He recognized the voice as that of Maxwell and, through the dark, could make out a figure. Maxwell said, "Up here. Reach for my hand." Maxwell had somehow managed to work his way up to the bottom of the boat and was hanging on to the shafts and rudders. He yelled for Lowe to reach for his hand. Lowe's foul-weather coat was soaked with water and was weighing him down and making it very difficult to move. He quickly removed his coat and tossed it aside. Without this weight, he was more buoyant, and as he reached up again, Maxwell grabbed his hand and pulled him up.

Lowe asked Maxwell if he had seen Murray and was told no. They both started to yell out Murray's name; and shortly, off the stern, they heard him yelling back to them. They could barely make him out and asked him to try to come toward their voices. Murray was soon alongside the forty-footer as Maxwell stretched out a leg, which Murray grabbed and seemed to climb right up. All three of them huddled together on the stern of the forty-footer not knowing what to do next. Every movement now had to be forced, and they were rapidly losing their strength. It seemed that all options had run out for them, and that it would just be a matter of time before the *CG-40564* sank, and they succumbed to the elements.

Edwards, on the *CG-36454*, saw the forty-footer disappear ahead of him; he got a very lonely feeling. He still had the company of his crew: Fireman Johnson and Seaman Croker. He knew that they must have been scared and feeling the same as he was. Edwards told everyone to make sure their life jackets were secure and, no matter what, to hang on. Just as he got these words out, the *CG-36454* was engulfed with a wall of water, perhaps the same one that would capsize the *CG-40564* ahead of them. Edwards hung on to the wheel as tightly as he could. The breaker landed right in the middle of the boat, and out of control, the boat was taken quite a distance with the wave. When the boat emerged from the wave, Edwards quickly looked around and saw both of his crew still aboard and hanging on to handgrips attached to the cabin structure. The boat seemed to be heading in the opposite direction and into the oncoming swells. Edwards did not know if they had capsized or pitch-poled the boat, but everything seemed to be operating normally; and he continued, at a slow bell, into the seas to gather his wits.

On the *Mermaid*, the Bergman brothers must have been terrified when they saw the *Triumph* disappear at the other end of the towline. The swell seemed to break between the *Triumph* and *Mermaid* with about twelve feet of white water hitting the *Mermaid*. The towline was suddenly brought taught, and with a loud bang, it parted at the bow of the *Mermaid*. They received a call from the *Triumph* stating that they were coming around to pass them the towline again. Right in front of them, they were horrified to see the *Triumph* start into the turn, and at the same time, a large breaker broke right over the lifeboat. She capsized and remained in that position. The Bergmans went out onto the after deck and heard, close to the side of the *Mermaid*, a call for help. They looked over the side and found a *Triumph* crew member, Engineer Petrin, reaching up for help. They quickly leaned over and brought him aboard. Other than being soaked, he seemed to be okay. They looked around and hollered for any more survivors but found none. All three then went into the cabin where Petrin asked to use the radio. He called the cape's tower, and Chief Porter answered. Petrin told him that the *Triumph* went over and had not righted herself, and he was the only one left. He pleaded for someone to come and get them and finished with "God help us." The chief told him that help was on the way in the form of two thirty-six-foot lifeboats from Point Adams and for them to do what they could, in the meantime, to save themselves.

It was heartbreaking for the people in the cape's tower and in the office at Point Adams and anyone in the surrounding area to listen to what was going on. This was really the first indication from anyone that boats and crews were down on the bar. At 8:00 PM, in anticipation of what might be needed, Chief Berto at Point Adams directed the lifeboat crews to man their boats, and they were underway shortly. BM1 Miller on the *CG-36535* would be heading directly to the bar area, and BM1 Lopez would head in the same direction but would divert to the cape's boathouse and pick up BM1 Webb.

Onboard the *Mermaid*, the Bergmans were doing their best by using their engine and propeller to go forward or astern when they thought they could avoid the breakers. They felt that they had unwillingly been brought into this situation and were just about helpless to do anything about it. Things were looking grim to them and Petrin. Looking out toward where they thought the lightship was located, the Bergman's noticed some lights they identified as the pilot boat *Peacock*. They quickly called the *Peacock*, and when Messer came up on the radio, they pleaded for him to come over and give them a line. Messer told them he could not reach their present position. He told them to maneuver the best way they could south and toward the range lights. If they could get closer to the channel, then maybe he could reach them.

The *CG-36454* with Edwards and his crew were blindly heading into the swells, trying to figure out what might be the best thing to do next. Edwards felt the bow rise, and as it did, he throttled up and went over the top as it broke beneath him. The boat came down and landed with a loud crack that put them all to their knees. As they recovered from this, they heard loud yelling coming from over the portside. Edwards looked over and could not believe what he was seeing. The *CG-36454*, after coming through the breaker, had landed square in the middle of the capsized *CG-40564*. Hanging on to the bottom of the *CG-40564*, the crew of the overturned forty-footer suddenly saw a huge object coming through the darkness toward them. The thirty-six footer landed on the forty-footer, narrowly missing the three crewman desperately hanging on. The men recognized the boat to be a thirty-six footer, and as it backed off, they thought that they had missed their opportunity to be saved.

When Lowe saw the thirty-six footer back away from them, he had decided that it was not going anywhere without him. Somehow, he drew from that inner strength; and before he even realized what he was doing, he stood up and dove off the forty-footer in the direction of the lifeboat. In short order, he reached the side and grabbed the lifelines hanging from the lifeboat's side. He held a death grip on the lifelines as he yelled for help from whoever might hear him. It seemed to him that the crew of the lifeboat did not seem to realize that they happened onto the forty-footer. Very quickly, Lowe felt strong hands grab his arms and pull him upward and into the forward well deck. This was when Lowe recognized his fellow shipmates from the cape and realized that this lifeboat was the *CG-36454*. As Edwards kept the boat clear of the forty-foot boat, everyone yelled to Maxwell and Murray to swim over to the side of the *CG-36454*. Edwards had no doubt that there had been some severe damage done to the lifeboat, and the first thing needed to be done was to get the others from the forty-footer over and aboard the lifeboat. He did not want to risk further contact with the forty-footer. Maxwell was the next to swim over and be hoisted aboard. When they yelled for Murray to swim over, he yelled back something about giving him the end of the towline so he could tie it to the *CG-40564*. What he wanted to do was tie a lifejacket to the other end of the line so that the forty-footer could later be found and salvaged. It was truly remarkable that any of those involved in the forty-footer capsizing were still alive. Everyone on the thirty-six footer told Murray, in no uncertain terms, to get his butt over to them now! Murray slipped off the forty-footer and swam as quickly as he could, and in short order, he was onboard the lifeboat.

Edwards picked up the radio handset, said mayday three times, and stated that he had three survivors from the *CG-40564* onboard; and that he thought his boat was in a sinking condition, and that he was making headway for the lightship. As Edwards was sending the mayday, he looked up at his boat's antenna and noticed half of it was gone. He hoped his signal had gotten out. In the cape's tower, Chief Porter had received the message from the *CG-36454* and felt some relief considering everything that had happened so far.

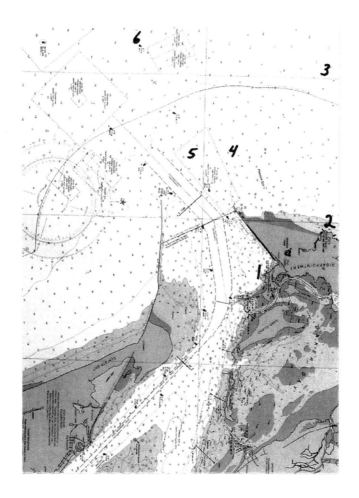

1. Cape Disappointment lookout tower.
2. North Head lighthouse.
3. Reported location (taken from official Assistance Reports of Cape Disappointment)of Mermaid in 90 ft. of water west of North Head Lt. when she was taken in tow by the CG-40564.
4. Peacock Spit area.
5. Location of unlighted Can Buoy #5 in 1961.
6. Buoy #1

Crew of 36 foot MLB wearing Kapok lifejackets. Note how
bulky and cumbersome they might be.

17

Trapped

Chief Porter now needed all the help he could find. Things had developed so fast that he had not had a chance to inform his superiors as to what had been going on. He picked up the phone and called his group commander, Chief Warrant Officer J. S. Breschini at Hoquiam, Washington. He quickly gave him a rundown, and Breschini told him to call the district and request anything he needed and that he would be down to the cape in a couple of hours. Chief Porter had the switchboard hook him up with RCC (rescue coordinating center) at the Thirteenth District offices in Seattle, Washington. In short order, he was talking to the duty officer at RCC and informed him on what was going on. The duty officer told him that he was alerting the air station at Port Angeles, Washington, to get a suitable aircraft underway to illuminate the area as needed. He also said that as they spoke, he had diverted another aircraft that was on a training mission from San Francisco to Port Angeles. The duty officer had also sent messages to the Coast Guard Cutter *Yocona* at Astoria, Oregon, and CGC *Modoc* at Coos Bay, Oregon, directing them to get underway as soon as possible and proceed to the distress area. When the *Yocona* arrived on scene, she was to act as on-scene commander coordinating the search. The officer of the deck at RCC was really ahead of the game as he had also been monitoring the situation on the district's radios. He had drafted up messages before hand and had open lines to the air station. He told Chief Porter that help was on the way and for Porter and Berto to do what they could on their end.

As Messer took the *Peacock* out to sea and around the middle ground to attempt the inbound run along the black line, the radio came alive again. "Mayday, mayday, mayday, this is the *CG-36454*. We have picked up three survivors from the *CG-40564*. We are in a sinking condition and attempting to reach the lightship."

On the bridge of the *Peacock*, there was over eighty years of at-sea experience in all conditions. Other than Messer with fifteen years, there was a licensed captain who was a bar pilot. There was also a licensed engineer and two deckhands with many years of experience. With all the factors weighed in, a decision was quickly made to turn around and try to find the *CG-36454* coming out the red buoy line. This was most likely a very wise decision. If the *Peacock* had ventured down the black line, she might have met the same fate as her sister ship on her maiden voyage south in 1943 as a commissioned navy minesweeper. As described earlier, due to inclement weather conditions, an attempt to seek refuge inside the Coos Bay, Oregon, entrance resulted in her loss along with thirteen of her crew.

Inside the aft berthing area when the *Triumph* capsized, Huggins was in the dark and bewildered as to why, when she went over, she did not right herself. He like many others had been told that the *Triumph* was built to be self-righting. He seemed to be uninjured and started to grope around for the battle lantern he knew was hanging from a bulkhead. Everything that was in the after compartment that was not secured, such as the spare towline, was now on the overhead, which was now the deck. Huggins finally found the lantern and turned it on to see that things were very unfamiliar with the upheaval of everything. Where the ladder up to the main deck had been, it was now a passageway down to the doghouse door, which was under water now. There were several feet of water now in this area. Huggins was trapped with no way out. It is hard to imagine what was going through his mind other than just being terrified. His position must have felt similar to one being buried alive. He stated later that, to the best of his recollection, the *Triumph* remained capsized for around twenty minutes, which had seemed like a lifetime to Huggins. All of a sudden, Huggins heard what must have been a breaker come down on the bottom; the *Triumph* shuddered and took a roll and came upright. When she righted herself, the door to the doghouse fell off the hinges. Huggins felt a rush of fresh air come down into the compartment, and he wasted no time climbing the ladder to get out of where he had been trapped. Once on deck, he quickly assessed the situation the best he could with the lantern he had brought up with him from below. He found no one on deck, and other than the breaking seas around him and the wind howling, there was complete silence.

He quickly opened the doghouse door to the engine room, thinking that he might restart the engine, and saw several feet of water. He knew it would have been futile to try. Even as Huggins thought about this, he did not know if he had the courage to enter that compartment. He shut the door and dogged it down as tight as he could. Huggins worked his way forward along the engine room cover to the coxswain's area. What he found around the pilothouse door to the forward compartment was a twisted mass of metal.

The seas had taken the top spray shield and collapsed it, making it impossible to open the door to that compartment. He pounded on the cabin door, hoping to hear anything from those that might be inside but heard nothing in return. The *Triumph* seemed to be riding very low in the water as Huggins made his way aft toward the doghouse where he found what he thought might be the safest place to take refuge. He lay down alongside the aft doghouse holding on to anything he could. In this position, he reached down and retightened all the straps on his life jacket.

Huggins, while hunkered down, thought he heard a call for help from somewhere out in the darkness. He yelled in return but heard nothing back. He was wet and cold and felt very lonely. He wondered about his shipmates and of what might be in store for him. As long as the boat gave him some sort of protection, he would remain with her until he had to leave or was washed off the deck. Every once in a while, he could see lights that he thought were the lighthouses at the cape and North Head. From his position relative to the lights, he thought that the boat must have been drifting north and close to or in Peacock Spit. Every once in a while, a breaker would come crashing down around the *Triumph*, but luckily nothing for the time being was directly hitting her.

18

Safe Haven

On the *Peacock*, Messer located the lights of the *CG-36454* west of buoy 2 and fell in behind her as close as possible. The thirty-six footer looked to be riding low in the stern but was, otherwise, making good speed toward the lightship. After the *CG-36454* had picked up the survivors of the *CG-40564* and given Lowe and Murray life jackets, Edwards put the throttle full ahead and set course out the red buoy line. They took a real beating until they reached a position around buoy 2. Edwards was worried that the stern compartment was full of water, and when Lowe cracked open the engine compartment door, he found the water level almost up to the engine air intake. It really gave them some relief when they saw the lights of the *Peacock* closely off their stern. Now, if anything happened, at least they would have a fighting chance at survival; but for now, they chose to run full throttle for the lightship.

When the *CG-36454* reached the lightship, Messer stopped the *Peacock* close by and made ready to pick up anyone that was unlucky enough to fall into the water. With the *Peacock*'s searchlight illuminating the area, the *CG-36454* made the approach to the lightship with difficulty. The water in her bilges was making her sluggish to answer the helm. The wind had lessened somewhat, but the seas were running fifteen to twenty feet.

There appeared to be some damage occurring in the lightship side of the thirty-six footer with parts of the gunwale tearing away. As the *CG-36454* rode to the top of a swell, one man jumped for the Jacob's ladder. A Jacob's ladder is one that is commonly used to board and disembark from ships to smaller boats. It is made of line with wood steps interwoven at every foot. Those on the *Peacock* watched in horror at what appeared to be a ladder rung that broke under the feet of a man; he was hanging by his arms.

The man hanging from the ladder was Terry Lowe of the *CG-40564*. Terry had spent a lot of time aboard lightships; he was very familiar with how to board and disembark using the Jacob's ladder. When reaching for and deciding to go up the ladder, one would want to attempt this at the top of a swell and quickly climb the rest of the way to safety. Any other way and you would risk the vessel you were leaving coming against the hull of the other vessel and trapping you between them. A direct blow would, most likely, not be survivable.

As Lowe hung there in imminent danger, someone on the *CG-36454* grabbed the throttle and put it in gear to keep the boat away from Lowe. This was one of the efforts that, most likely, saved Lowe's life once again. Lowe had nearly lost his life several times that night, and by this time, he was very weak and seemed unable to help himself any further. Later, Lowe was to learn that the person who grabbed the throttle to back the thirty-six footer away from possibly fatally injuring him was BM1 Murray.

When Lowe looked up, he saw the head of this man with outstretched arms reaching down for him. This man was later identified as the new commanding officer, CWO Ray Johnson, who had just come aboard earlier that day from the MLB *Triumph*. When the lightship had first heard that the *CG-36454* was headed their way, Johnson had his crew make ready with lines out and Jacob ladders available. When Johnson was on deck directing the rescue effort for those from the *CG-36454*, he saw what happened with Lowe; and before he realized what he was doing, he hooked a safety line around him and got down on his knees above the Jacob's ladder where Lowe was hanging. Johnson directed his crew to take the end of his safety line and grab his feet. Suddenly, Johnson was hanging head down, reaching for Lowe. He grabbed Lowe by his wrists and hollered to his crew "Got him." In another instant, the lightship crew pulled Lowe and Johnson to safety.

A new Jacobs's ladder had been put in place of the broken one, lines had been passed to the *CG-36454*, and as she rode up and down and in quick succession, the five remaining men made it safely aboard the lightship. After everyone was aboard the lightship, the *Peacock* returned to her station off buoy 1 and prepared to work on a couple of outbound freighters. She would remain outside until around 7:00 AM, awaiting better visibility and sea conditions on the bar.

In the cape's tower, Chief Porter had received a call from the lightship letting him know that his men were all safely onboard the ship. This was another slight relief for him. The words Chief Porter had heard from Petrin kept coming back to him. They would haunt Porter for the rest of his life as it did many others. He felt helpless to do anything, and it was a terrible temptation to go down to the boathouse and get underway with the only boat he had left, the *CG-40421*. However, his experience and common sense held him back as the *CG-40421* was another forty-footer similar to the *CG-40564* that had already been lost.

BM1 Webb had, shortly before, left the tower to go down to the station area. The first thing he did before going to the boathouse to get aboard the *CG-36554* was to get Meyer and Dillard headed for Benson Beach to search for survivors. They took the cape's jeep, which had a radio, and left. At 8:45 PM, Webb arrived at the boathouse; and while waiting for the *CG-36554* to arrive, he also took note of the *CG-40421* sitting at the dock. Like Porter, he understood that if he were to be of any assistance and bring his crew through, it would be with the thirty-six-foot lifeboat. He looked out the channel and saw the lights of the thirty-six footer coming in, and he went down to the end of the dock to wait.

19

U.S. Coast Guard Cutter *Yocona*

At 4:00 PM on 12 January 1961, the Coast Guard Cutter *Yocona* was secured at her moorage on the face of pier 1 in Astoria, Oregon. Liberty had just been granted to sections 2 and 3. The *Yocona* was a deep-sea tug and one of the largest of her kind, measuring 213 foot in length. She was a diesel-electric ship with two engine rooms: B-1 and B-2. B-1 had two Cooper-Bessemer diesel engines that provided drive to the generators in B-2 that gave power to the twin electric drive motors.

She originally was built for the U.S. Navy in 1944 as a salvage ship of the Diver class. In 1946, she was transferred to the Coast Guard and was given the name Yocona. In 1950, she was home ported at Astoria, Oregon, to serve as a medium-endurance cutter for search-and-rescue and other marine duties. She had a compliment of seven officers and sixty-eight enlisted men. Commanding officer during 1960 and 1961 was Commander William G. Blandford.

At 8:20 PM, the officer of the day received a phone call from the Rescue Coordination Center, Thirteenth District, Seattle. This call alerted the *Yocona* to the circumstances that had and were taking place on the Columbia River bar. The *Yocona* was directed to proceed as soon as possible to the area and, upon arrival, assume on-scene commander. Under this status, the *Yocona* would coordinate and direct all vessels and aircraft being deployed in the search-and-rescue efforts. At the same time the *Yocona* received the message, so did the Coast Guard Cutter *Modoc* at Coos Bay, Oregon, a couple hundred miles south. The *Modoc* was a 143-foot ex-Navy fleet tug. The ship was transferred to the Coast Guard and served the area as a medium-endurance cutter in the same manner as the *Yocona* at Astoria. The *Modoc* would steam all night in large seas to arrive the next morning at 11:00 AM. The rescue center at Seattle wanted the *Modoc* underway for use as a backup for the *Yocona* if needed.

The officer of the deck on the *Yocona* directed the quartermaster to commence a recall of as many of the crew that could be located. Engineer First Class Jerry Glien proceeded to B-1 engine room to light off the main engines. Glien had a new fireman apprentice with him, and in short, order they had both engines operating and warming up. He was informed by the OOD to let him know when the engines were warm enough to get underway as they would leave at that time. Due to the nature of this call, the *Yocona* would leave the pier with a skeleton crew. It would be approximately thirty minutes from the time the call was received that the last lines were off, and the *Yocona* maneuvered from the pier into the shipping lanes. Her logs read 9:08 PM; course was set to conform to the Columbia River channel en route to the river entrance at eight knots. The anemometer on the *Yocona* was registering consistent winds out of the west-southwest at near gale or thirty-two to thirty-eight knots. It would take the *Yocona* approximately one hour to get to the search area on the bar.

Commander Blandford was receiving constant radio traffic from RCC, Westport Radio, and the local stations, updating him on conditions of the bar area as other units were getting underway. As soon as all the mooring lines were put below and the decks secure, Commander Blandford ordered all weather decks secured until further notice. This meant that no one would be allowed to venture outside of the ship's house. There was a very real danger of being washed overboard. Throughout the night, the ship would be taking seas as high as the wings of the bridge. As the *Yocona* was steaming outbound, things were happening at the Coast Guard air station, Port Angeles, Washington. In 1961, the nearest USCG air station to the mouth of the Columbia River was at Port Angeles, approximately seventy-five miles east of Tatoosh Island in the Straits of Juan de Fuca. At this air station were several twin-engine seaplanes of the UF Albatross class. They had been the mainstay of the air wing of the U.S. Coast Guard for many years. There was a love-hate kind of relationship between the UFs and those that flew in them. They were very noisy inside and out. It was possible to hear one coming for miles. If an engine failed at take off, the pilot needed to be very ready to compensate. Several of these aircraft have been lost over the years, and it was mostly due to human error with some losses due to mechanical failure.

Coast Guard Cutter Yocona in the configuration and color she was in 1961.

20

Mermaid in Tow for the Third Time

It was at around 8:30 PM when BM1 Miller and Lopez, on Point Adams's thirty-six-foot motor lifeboat, were heading outbound when they overheard the conversation about the *Triumph* capsizing. When they passed buoy 19, Miller noticed that the *CG-36554* had veered off to the right some and had set course for the channel entrance into Baker Bay to pick up BM1 Webb at the cape's boathouse. Even a mile or two upriver from the bar area, Miller could feel small swells crossing under the boat. He knew that there was a ship ahead of him by the name off the SS *Diaz de Solis*, and he picked up the radio to give them a call. Bar pilot Captain Kenneth McAlpin came back to him. McAlpin stated to Miller that his office told him that due to the search-and-rescue case going on in the bar area, if possible, he should turn around and anchor. He also stated that he was committed to continuing outbound because it was now unsafe to attempt a turn. McAlpin told Miller that he would be going dead slow with just enough speed so he could keep the ship in the area as long as possible. This way, he would be able to use the ship's searchlight to help the *CG-36535* locate the *Mermaid* or survivors from the *Triumph*.

At 9:00 PM, Miller and his crew sighted what appeared to be the stern light of the *Diaz de Solis* a short distance ahead. Miller veered off to his right enough to clear the starboard side of the ship, and as he did so, he watched the ship's searchlight scanning the area to the northwest. It was not long until Miller spotted something in the light's beam about one-quarter mile away. They identified it as the *Mermaid*, and Miller headed in that direction at full speed, riding over very large swells and managing to make it over the crests before any of them broke. The time was 9:15 PM, and as the *CG-36535* arrived alongside the *Mermaid*, the *CG-36554* had picked up BM1 Webb and was heading outbound at best speed.

The *CG-36535* approached the *Mermaid* as close as possible and saw that Engineer Petrin was on the bow ready to receive the towline. Miller, as soon as he arrived, gave consideration to try to remove the people from the *Mermaid* but soon gave up on this as a couple of twenty-five- to thirty-foot breakers roared by. The towline on the *CG-36535* was still the old three-and-a-half-inch manila line.

As Miller went by the bow, one of his crew threw a small heaving line that was attached to the larger towline. It landed directly across the bow of the *Mermaid*. Petrin quickly pulled the towline over, and it was secured through the bow chock on a large cleat on the *Mermaid*. Miller's crew let out the towline as he quickly put some distance between the *CG-36535* and the *Mermaid*. When he looked back and thought it was enough, he told them to make it fast, which they did.

Conditions were not getting any better, and so far, the *Mermaid* had managed to avert any large breakers that would do major damage. It was almost unimaginable that the *Mermaid* and those aboard her had survived this long under these conditions. Miller really had nowhere to go with the *Mermaid* but to try to get across the bar in a direct course out the red buoy line toward the lightship. The ship off to their side was illuminating the waters ahead of Miller; and this did help some in seeing, in advance, what might be coming at him. He saw an awful lot of white water all around him, which he didn't mind as much; it was the ones that were building up to break that he needed to avoid.

The first aircraft, the *UF-1273*, was on a training flight north from San Francisco and reported in to the CGC *Yocona* at 9:30 PM. The *UF-1273* stated that they would be in the area within the next twenty minutes. *Yocona* directed the *UF-1273* to drop flares starting offshore from North Head Lighthouse and along a southerly direction across the river entrance.

At 9:45 PM, Miller and the *CG-36535* were experiencing great difficulties with the tow. They had narrowly missed several very large plunging breakers. All of a sudden, the bow of the *CG-36535* rose sharply; Miller pushed the throttle forward as much as he felt would be necessary to push them over the top of the swell. The *CG-36535* barely made it over the top when the swell started to break. The swell was concave on the backside, and as the *CG-36535* came over the top, there was nothing but air beneath her. As the bow pointed in a downward direction, the boat rolled to the starboard, and she slammed violently on her side in the trough of the wave.

All three crew members were knocked to their knees and, losing their grips on handholds, were piled together on the deck and under the starboard catwalk. The boat quickly recovered as did the crew, and then they found that they no longer had the *Mermaid* in tow. As Miller tried to keep the boat and crew out of any further trouble, his crew quickly pulled in what was left of the towline.

Onboard the *Mermaid*, the Bergmans and Petrin, after securing the towline, quickly returned to the back area of the cabin. The *CG-36535* had them in tow for about twenty minutes, and it seemed that they would never get out of the mess they had been in for several hours now. As they peered through the forward windows, they could see the *CG-36535* about two hundred feet in front of them, and as they watched, the thirty-six footer rose up in a vertical angle while climbing up a huge wave. The *CG-36535* seemed to jump over the top with its stern up into the air. They must have looked on in horror as the wave that the lifeboat had just gone over crested and broke completely over the top of the *Mermaid*. Onboard the *Diaz de Solis*, the pilot was watching things unfold in the beam of the searchlight. He saw the *CG-36535* go over this huge wave (later said to be forty to forty-five foot by Miller) followed by it cresting and crashing over the *Mermaid*. When the wave had rolled on by, there was no sign of the *Mermaid* or those on board. Concurrently the ship's searchlight burned out, and Pilot McAlpin said that for the safety of his ship, he had to proceed outbound. Miller and his crew quickly made a search of the area but could find nothing.

A short time later, Webb with the *CG-36554* arrived on the bar and had located the *CG-36535*. The *Yocona* was on the bar also by this time and directed the two thirty-six footers to commence a search along the red line between buoys 6 and 12. This area skirted Clatsop Spit, another very dangerous area, and the *Yocona* would later direct the lifeboats to search a little further upriver. Aboard the *CG-36554*, Webb and his crew were keeping a sharp eye and ear out for anything. Webb had previously spent over six years with the Coast Guard on the Columbia River. He had not seen conditions this bad on the bar. He has since stated that it would be many years before he saw anything worse than what he saw that night.

21

The Angels Are Coming

Upon arrival on the bar area, Commander Blandford sent messages to the district commander and all units involved. This message stated the time of their arrival and that he had assumed as on-scene commander. All units responding from this point would be under the control of the *Yocona*, and Blandford would direct each unit in the search. He had been informed of the capsizing of the *Triumph* and the loss of the *CG-40564*. He was told that the *CG-36454* had rescued the crew of the *CG-40564*, and that everyone was safely aboard the lightship with the *CG-36454* tied astern. This left Blanford with the search for any survivors of the *Triumph* and the *Mermaid*. The *CG-36554* and *CG-36535* were on the bar awaiting directions from Blandford.

The *Yocona* had commenced a search using their carbon arc searchlights, which could scan an area of up to a half-mile around their position. Blandford could see and feel the terrible conditions around him. He was not well versed on the use and operation of Coast Guard lifeboats, but he had heard many stories about the boats and the men who operated them. He also realized that the men onboard the lifeboats wanted desperately to find and save their shipmates and missing fishermen if at all possible. From what Blanford had seen and heard, he made the decision to have the two lifeboats run search patterns from just inside the bar. Due to the tide flooding during most of this case, there was a possibility that some survivors might be in that area. Another of his reasons for deciding on this particular search pattern was that if the *Yocona* or an aircraft sighted something, the lifeboats would be close enough to investigate. It would not be worth it to jeopardize the lifeboats and men any further unless there was a confirmed sighting on the bar or in Peacock Spit.

For the U.S. Coast Guard Air Station Port Angeles, the first indication that there was a problem down the coast was at approximately 8:50 PM when the district office in Seattle contacted the air station and requested an aircraft. They would be needed to drop illumination flares for an ongoing case at the mouth of the Columbia River. The *UF-1273* had been on a training flight from San Francisco for Port Angeles and was contacted to divert to the Columbia River entrance. The *UF-1273* would arrive on scene at 9:30 PM and would be directed by the *Yocona* to drop flares. At the same time, the alarm was sounded at the air station to ready the crews of the *UF-1240* and *UF*-2131 to depart.

There was a quick meeting of the air crews, and they were informed that there had been several Coast Guard boats and personnel lost at the entrance to the Columbia River. The aircraft departed as soon as ready on a southwest course, climbing to an altitude to clear the Olympic Mountains. Onboard the *UF-1240* were AL2 (aviation electronics) Al Lucas and AD2 (aviation machinist mate) John Amiot, the only two enlisted members along with the pilot and copilot. Lucas was the electronics man aboard responsible for the radios, radar, and direction-finder equipment. Amiot was the flight mechanic responsible for the overall mechanics of the aircraft. On search-and-rescue cases, crew members worked at all jobs on the aircraft, and they depended on each other. On long flights, it was not uncommon for the pilot or copilot to relinquish their seat to give the other crew members some supervised time at the controls.

Somewhere behind the *UF-1240* was the *UF-2131*, and as they cleared the Olympic Mountains, the pilots set a course that would take them to the entrance of the Columbia River. At the same time, the *UF-1240* started a slow descent that would bring them to 4,500 feet over the target area for parachute flare drops. Lucas and Amiot busied themselves, getting into their safety harnesses and the flares ready for launching. When on scene, they would be informed by the pilot when to launch the flares. Amiot would be at the port rear door that he could open, and Lucas would drop from a door that opened upward on the starboard side directly across from Amiot. Both would have their safety harnesses hooked to the inside framework of the aircraft.

As they neared the coast, the storm brewing outside was very noticeable, and the *UF-1240* was buffeted all over the place. Visibility was poor, and rain pounded the aircraft. When they arrived on scene, Lucas would arm the flares that Amiot would be dropping, and Amiot would then arm Lucas's flares. These flares, once armed, had to be used; and a lanyard would be hooked to it so that when dropped and well clear of the aircraft, it would break loose of the lanyard and ignite. A Coast Guard Albatross was lost a few years later with all hands over the Gulf of Mexico when a flare accidently ignited inside the cabin. Arming and dropping the flares was a highly dangerous job and took teamwork to bring the exercise off safely.

At 10:15 PM, the *UF-1240* came down in the area to 4,500 feet, heading in as closely as possible parallel to the coast and about one mile offshore. The pilots had contacted the *UF-1273*, and they worked with each other on a separate frequency, coordinating their own search to avoid possible collisions. In other words, the aircrafts acted as their own air controllers. They also checked in with the *Yocona* and were advised on the present situation and of what their duties should be.

The wind was coming hard from the southwest, and any airdrops were expected to drift right over the area where any survivors might be. Both crew members opened their respective doors, and the noise from the weather and engines outside was almost deafening even though both men were wearing headsets. The pilot came over the headsets telling them to standby, and Amiot reached over to Lucas and armed his flare. Lucas did the same for him, and they stood ready for the pilot's command to drop.

Aboard the *Triumph*, Huggins was hanging on to anything he could get hold of with hands that were fast becoming stiff from the cold. By this time, what we now know as hypothermia was in its advanced stages, and it would not be long before he would not be able to help himself at all. It seemed to him that it had been hours since he had gotten free of the aft compartment when the *Triumph* righted. He was downright scared and had every reason to be. All around him, it had been white water with an occasional wave washing over the *Triumph* that threatened to take him overboard.

By this time, Huggins was sure that he was in Peacock Spit as he could see the cape's lighthouse almost straight ahead toward what he thought was shore. Facing the cape's light, there was another light directly to his left that he assumed was North Head. If the lights were what he thought, then he believed that he was very close to shore. He knew he was not thinking very clearly by this time, and that the angels were coming to get him. He could see this light above him; and almost hypnotically, he stared at it and, at the same time, felt very serene. Because of the storm and the altitude from where the aircraft were dropping flares, he did not realize that the light he saw was flares.

Suddenly, there was a jolt, and the *Triumph* rolled at a sharp angle. At the same time, a wave came across the deck and washed Huggins overboard.

111

He found himself in the water hardly able to move his limbs to help himself. Luckily, his life jacket was still well secured, including the collar around his neck. Secured properly, the jacket would keep his head above water, and even though he would be unable to help himself much, he could survive for some time yet. He had not been in the water very long when he felt his feet hit the bottom. He was in very shallow water now, and the waves were a lot smaller and seemed to be carrying him toward the beach. His senses were somewhat coming back to him, and he thought he saw a dim light in the darkness. He started yelling for help as loud as he could.

Meyer and Dillard had made their way in the cape's jeep to the driftwood area on Benson Beach. This beach ran two miles from the north jetty to North Head light. The beach was all sandy down to North Head where several jagged rocks reached a short distance seaward from the Head. They left the jeep close to a beach access and proceeded on foot with flashlights. They had decided to leave the jeep because the tide was high, and there did not seem to be a lot of area between the driftwood and water. They had not gone very far when they thought they heard something. They stopped and strained to hear. Faintly, they heard someone calling for help up the beach toward North Head. They hurriedly headed in that direction and were surprised, after only going a short distance, to hear the voice calling directly from the sea.

They carefully threaded their way through loose driftwood floating about in the direction where they thought they heard the voice. When they were in water up to their knees, they spotted something ahead of them. In a few quick steps, they found Huggins lying in the water. They grabbed Huggins, and it was a strain to haul him farther up the beach to a drier area above the waterline. They made a quick assessment of him and found that, with their support, he could stand and walk. As quickly as possible, they assisted Huggins to the jeep and got him into the passenger side. While one drove, the other got on the radio and called the cape to tell them that they had found Huggins alive and in fair shape. They were told to transport him to the local hospital in Ilwaco, Washington, which was three to four miles away. It did not take Meyer and Dillard long before they got Huggins to the hospital, and they were on their way back to continue searching the beach area.

Benson Beach looking south from North Head Lt. house.

Benson Beach looking north from the North Head light along
Benson beach.

22

Danger in the Air

Aboard the *UF-1240*, unlike the pilot and copilot who were strapped into their seats, both of the crew members were barely maintaining their balance with so much turbulence. Amiot was to drop his flare first, and about ten seconds later, Lucas would drop his. It was not long before the pilot called over the intercom and told them to drop. Amiot immediately dropped his and yelled, "Flare away." Lucas counted to himself to ten and put his flare out the door. As he did, he immediately turned away from the hatch so that the ignition would not affect his night vision.

He turned around to pick up another flare and to arm Amiot's, but to his horror—as he looked over to where Amiot was supposed to be—all he saw was the lower half of his body inside the door. Lucas, at the time, was a very trim 160 lbs; and Amiot had just barely passed his flight physical at 235 lbs. The only thing holding Amiot to the aircraft was his safety harness. Lucas's harness had just enough play in it, allowing him to get over and grab Amiot's legs.

The pilot heard Lucas yelling over the intercom and turned his head to look back. He could not believe what he saw. He immediately put the aircraft into a shallow dive to lessen the strain on Lucas in trying to get Amiot back inside the plane. It was with great effort that Lucas was able to pull him back in. As soon as he was inside, both men set to the task of dropping flares. Lucas had always heard that Amiot had nerves of steel but could not believe how calm he was after what had just occurred. The aircraft had been buffeted around so much that just as Amiot put a flare out, the plane took a violent roll to the port. Amiot was caught off balance and was ejected partially out the door as far as his harness would allow. Amiot, in the future, would stay as far away from the opening as he could and still perform his duties. Amiot looked at Lucas with a big smile on his face. Lucas yelled at him, "Don't do that again!" The rest of the night,

Lucas could not help but keep one eye on himself and one eye on Amiot. As the aircraft's made their runs along the coast, they would do so in an oval configuration, and the direction and spacing would be decided between the aircraft's pilots to avoid midair collisions.

As the *UF-1240* made the turn out to sea and backup the coast for another run, they could see the flares they had dropped slowly drifting down to sea. They could also see the running lights of the other aircrafts and the flares that they were dropping.

Everyone aboard the aircraft knew that the only thing they could do was drop the flares in the hopes that it would aid in the search for survivors. What they did not know was that on the boats below, the men were searching for what they all knew would be a fruitless effort after this much time had elapsed to find any survivors. The flare drops were very comfortable to these men. It helped them orient their search and, somehow, seemed to bring a little peace after such a tragic situation.

With three aircraft involved that terrible night, they would drop almost forty parachute flares in support of the ground and water searches going on below. All aircraft searches would be conducted during daylight hours for several days along the beaches in the area without any significant findings. A month or so later Al Lucas, being an electronics-type of person, was assigned the task of assisting electronic shops down the coast in the installation of ADFs (automatic direction finders) on a few selected boats.

At 10:43 PM, the *Yocona* was informed of the finding of Huggins on Benson Beach. They were also informed that the *Triumph* had been sighted capsized close to the beach in the same area. This was a statement taken directly from the *Yocona* logbook; all other logbooks made no mention of sightings of the *Triumph*. It was possible that there were sightings of what someone might have thought was the *Triumph* or the *Mermaid*. By this time, on both sides of the Columbia River, hundreds of locals had converged on the beaches to search.

After receiving word that Huggins had been found alive, Commander Blanford made the decision to take the *Yocona* across the bar and search north. Up to then, Blandford had kept the *Yocona* just inside the roughest part of the bar near buoy 12 and directed the units that were searching. He set course to a position between buoys 1 and 3 where, if conditions were appropriate, he would then turn to a northerly direction.

In the following days, there would be a Coast Guard investigation into the case, and Commander Blandford was asked why he did not take his ship in closer. It would seem that who ever asked this question was not well educated in the operation of large ships in close quarters with rough seas. Blandford stated that he was as close as he dared considering wind and sea conditions, and that he did not want to jeopardize his ship and crew. There was a reason why this area is called the Graveyard of the Pacific. There was also a reason why there is an assigned on-scene commander, and that is to coordinate the search between all units so that not everyone is going in different directions. The following message was sent to everyone involved in the search efforts.

12:00 AM
13 January 1961
From *Yocona* log:

Underway, standing out of the Columbia River entrance conducting search as On Scene Commander. Looking for approximately six persons, one fishing vessel and two Coast Guard boats. Two Coast Guard 36 footers, 2 Coast Guard UF2G aircraft and various beach parties aiding in search.

The *Yocona* search area is from one to three miles from shore commencing at Clatsop Spit and in a northerly direction.

The *Yocona* would continue searching and directing the efforts as per her message until the early-morning hours. During this period, the seas and bar remained very rough with seas approaching twenty to thirty feet and winds gusting to over fifty-five knots.

The engine room was most likely the best place to be on a ship as far as the ride went in rough seas. What was not the best were the smell of diesel and other oils. The heat could also make it most uncomfortable.

Engineer Glien and his fireman had been maintaining watch over the engines with Glien faring better. While the ship was heading into the seas or having them on the stern, the ride was barely tolerable. When the ship had the seas broadside or nearly so, the ride would be most grueling. Glien would later say that the overall ride that night was nasty and aggravating. The fireman had spent a lot of time losing his stomach in the bilge but managed to maintain his duties. On the bridge, Commander Blanford felt confident that so far he had made the right decisions. If the *Yocona* sighted anything, he would then make the decision on whether to bring in the lifeboats.

Grumman Albatross 1240 as she appeared 12 January 1961.
The 1240 was lost with all hands in the Gulf of Mexico in 1967.

23

Grim Discovery

About the time the *Yocona* was outbound, word was received that one victim had been found on Benson Beach. The victim would be identified as BM1 John Culp. When Huggins had been reported as found alive, Chief Porter chose to leave the tower and go back down to the main building. The group commander had shortly before arrived at the station, and Porter needed to get him updated on what was going on. When Porter arrived at the station, he was informed that members of the Ilwaco Fire Department search party had located a victim on Benson Beach. Chief Porter and the group commander left for the beach area to identify the remains. When they arrived, there was a group of people gathered around the victim who was lying face down on the beach. The victim was not wearing a lifejacket, but it was noted that there was one close by on the beach. Upon examination, it was found that all straps were tied as they should have been with the exception of the leg straps. Without the leg straps secured properly, these jackets could be pulled off the person trying to survive in breaking seas or the surf.

Chief Porter did not recognize the victim on the beach, but he reached down and found the victim's billfold in a back pocket. When he opened the billfold, he found the government ID card belonging to BM1 John L. Culp.

The firemen had a litter with them and placed Culp in it, and they were directed to transport him to Pentilla's Chapel by the Sea at Long Beach, Washington. It was a very sad duty that Chief Porter had to do in identifying Culp, and he could only imagine what Chief Berto was going through over at Point Adams.

All this time, Chief Berto had pretty much been left with only a couple of his crew members at Point Adams. He was very worried about his boat crews and the others out there. He was constantly pacing back and forth. Many of the local people had dropped by the station to offer their assistance.

Those that Berto thought were able were asked to go down to the beaches of Clatsop Spit and search for survivors. So far, Berto felt that everything had been kept from the wives of the married men on the *Triumph*, and this is how he wanted to keep it until more information came in.

He gave his wife, Rina, a call and informed her of what was going on. The chief asked Rina to get hold of Colleen Simonsen and work together with her on a plan that would support the wives of the crew members. Rina came by Colleen's house some time before 9:00 PM and told her that they thought something had happened to the *Triumph* and her crew. Rina told her not to say anything about what might be going on.

Colleen had been home all day and had the normal conversations with several of the Coast Guard wives. Judy Hoban had come over late in the afternoon saying that her husband, John, had gone out on the *Triumph*. She visited a while and left to go to a movie in Astoria. She told Colleen that she would return later if John had not returned yet. After Colleen told her that maybe Judy would stop by later, Rina told her not to just talk to her until she goes home.

Judy did arrive back shortly after 9:00 PM and stayed until around 11:00 PM. It was hard for Colleen not to reach out to her, knowing that maybe Judy had lost her husband that day. While Judy was there, Colleen received several phone calls from various townspeople and from Coast Guard wife, Joan Miller. All were either trying to find out what was going on or had some information to share. Colleen carefully answered questions but was able to make it clear that Judy was sitting right there so the caller would understand why Colleen had to be rather vague in her conversation. Joan Miller, for example, remembers that she called Colleen sometime that night and told her that she knew her husband, Paul Miller, was not on the *Triumph*.

When confirmation came that there was a possible loss of the *Triumph* and her crew, the locals started planning on what they could do to help and give comfort to those at Point Adams and their families. Howard and Colleen Simonsen would ensure that no wife would be left alone after being informed of the loss of her husband. Shortly after midnight, Point Adams was informed of the finding of BM1 Culp's body, and that the possibility of any other survivors from the Triumph other than Huggins was pretty slim.

Rina Berto returned to the station before midnight to retrieve any further information from her husband and ask him when he wanted the wives to be told about what had happened. She found her husband in the bathroom throwing up blood. Chief Berto had been suffering from a case of ulcers for some time now, and the stress of the night had finally gotten to him.

He was throwing up a good amount of blood, and she comforted him as best she could. He told her that the wives needed to be informed, which he wanted her to take care of. Berto said he was going to call LaVerne Culp's parents in Port Angeles, Washington, and let them know what had happened. Before Rina departed, Berto made this call and was told that they would leave right away and should be at Point Adams early in the morning.

The only good thing that happened to the crew of Point Adams that night was that both of the station's thirty-six-foot lifeboats and their crews would come through the ordeal okay. There was only minor damage to the boats; and their crews were roughed up but, otherwise, in good physical shape. Mentally, for the crews of both stations, there would be long-lasting effects that would stay with them for many years if not for the rest of their lives.

The two thirty-six-foot motor lifeboats had carefully been searching the area just inside the main channel along the outer edge of Clatsop Spit without any sightings of survivors or wreckage. The only noise they heard was from the engine exhausts and the occasional crash of large breakers in the spit. They would continue this search for several hours, and it gave everyone time to think about what had happened that night. This was especially true on the *CG-36535* with BM1 Miller and Seaman Ponton. Both of these men had duty that night, and except for some unforeseen circumstances, they most likely would have been aboard the *Triumph*. Everyone remained quiet in their thoughts about what they knew was, most likely, the loss of their shipmates.

At 12:40 AM, the beach patrols reported that a large amount of life jackets were coming into Benson Beach. The amount of life jackets showing up far exceeded the number that would have been worn by all the men. Most were stenciled with the name MLB *Triumph*. This would be an indication that the *Triumph*, most likely, had been broken open in the surf, releasing the many life jackets that were stowed inside.

It was around 1:00 AM when two of the aircraft reported to the *Yocona* that they would have to depart shortly due to lack of fuel and flares. Leaving one aircraft in the area, *Yocona* released the two UFs to return to Port Angeles, load up on fuel and flares, and standby until further notice.

Onboard the lightship, the crew had made the survivors as comfortable as possible. The first thing they did was put them into warm showers and gave them all dry clothes. Terry Lowe and the others, even while standing under the warm water flowing over their bodies, felt that they would never get warm again. They were all very lucky to be alive, especially those from the *CG-40564*. The men that took refuge on the lightship would remain there for another three days until the weather abated, and the pilot boat *Peacock* could get them off and back in across the bar.

1. Approximate position of MLB Triumph when she took over the tow from CG-40564 and then shortly lost the tow.
2. Approximate position of the Triumph and the CG-40564 when they were capsized.
3. Approximate position where CG-36454 came upon the capsized CG-40564 and rescued the three men that were clinging to the bottom.
4. Columbia River Lightship.
5. Approximate location of the Mermaid when she was taken in tow by the CG-36535. The Mermaid was shortly lost in this area.
6. Clatsop Spit area.
7. Gordon Huggins found alive on Benson Beach
8. BM1 Culp found deceased on Benson Beach.

24

Bad News to Bear

Joan Miller, the wife of Paul Miller, was walking home from the store, and while rounding a corner, she saw her husband standing in the middle of the street yelling for her to hurry up because he had to go on a call. As stated earlier, Joan had asked her husband if he could come home for a few minutes so she could go to the store. It was a little after 5:00 PM and was twilight out, which was rather typical of a winter night near the river. Joan does not remember it being so windy that she was alarmed that the station and her husband had a call. She thinks it was later that night, at around 9:00 PM, when she got a phone call from Virginia Perkins, the chief engineer's wife. Virginia asked her if Paul had duty that night, and Joan told her he did. Virginia said something was going on, but asked her not to call the station or anyone else. She said she would get back to Joan as soon as she found out anything else. Joan said that she did not even think of her husband and the other men being in a seriously dangerous situation on the boats.

The Miller's two sons were asleep, their TV was off because it did not work, and the thirteen-band radio was inoperative. This left everything very quiet as Joan paced back and forth in her bare feet, wondering what was going on. She did not have to wait long before Virginia called back. She said that a boat had gone over, and that some of the men were overboard. She knew that one of them was BM1 Culp but felt sure that Joan's husband was okay. She took the information at face value—that her husband was okay—and felt confident that the others were all right and would get out of whatever predicament they were facing.

A little after 11:00 PM, the phone rang, and it was Joan's mother-in-law from the Seattle area. They had just heard on the news that the *Triumph* had rolled over, and that some of the men were missing along with a crab boat and its crew. It seemed that her in-laws knew much more about what was going on than Joan did. Joan tried to reassure her mother-in-law that her son was okay. Then her father-in-law, Willis Miller, got on the phone as he was very upset. Both parents had been down to visit Hammond many times; and Miller's father, in particular, had become acquainted with some of the men. Willis said that he and Joy were getting ready and would be down as soon as they could the next day.

In Joan's mind, she knew that her husband, Paul, was okay and did everything she could to calm his parents down. It was shortly after that that Joan hung up the phone and continued pacing the floor. Around midnight, Peggy Enlund, the next-door neighbor to the Millers, came home. Peggy was the wife of David Enlund, the skipper of the pilot boat, *Peacock*. Peggy, seeing all the lights on at Joan's house, went over to the Miller house. Peggy had heard from her husband about events of that night. She was older than Joan and decided that she would stay with her until they found out more about what was really going on.

It was also about this time that both Rina Berto and Virginia Perkins came to the Miller house. They were just checking to see if someone was with Joan. Peggy assured them that she would stay with her until Paul or someone else came to stay.

Joan and Rina both knew that Lois Brooks had just returned from the hospital that day after losing her baby. Chief Berto had earlier sent BM2 Ron Brooks home so that he could be with his wife during this difficult time. Just west of the Miller house was the apartment where the Brooks lived, and looking in that direction, they could see that no lights appeared to be on. They both hoped that no one would disturb them because if Brooks knew something was going on, he would return to the station on his own. Earlier, Chief Berto had left orders that no one should disturb Brooks. Berto also was aware that he would be better off with a well-rested boatswain mate in the morning to assist at the station and possibly on a lifeboat.

Shortly after Rina and Virginia left the Miller home, Howard Simonsen came by. He told Peggy that he needed to take Joan for a quick ride and asked her to stay with the kids until they got back. They drove by the Brooks apartment and were assured that no lights were on. Then Howard told Joan that BM1 Culp's body had been found on Benson Beach.

Howard asked directions to the Culp's house, and then they drove by the Culp house as well. Joan recognized Virginia Perkins's car parked out front and knew that Virginia would be with LaVerne, her good friend.

Howard also told Joan that BM2 Hoban's wife was at their house, and that he was trying to make sure that no Coast Guard wife was left alone while all of this was going on. Howard and Colleen Simonsen were the closest friends of the Millers outside of the Coast Guard at Hammond. The Simonsens always looked after the Coast Guard families from Point Adams in many ways, and they continued do so as long as the lifeboat station remained in operation.

LaVerne Culp had heard nothing about what had been going on that night except that her husband had gone out on a call and would be home shortly. This was nothing new but a matter of routine at lifeboat stations. As for LaVerne Culp, she remembers that 12 January 1961 was a very windy day. As she had opened the laundry-room door, the wind caught it and ripped it off its hinges. The laundry room was just an addition to the house and could only be entered from the outside. She stated that she had stewed about this all day but was soon to learn that nothing material is worth worrying about.

As the evening went by, she began to feel a little bit uneasy about things but, finally, went in to shower and wash her hair. She had left every light on in the house and had been into and out of bed several times. Finally, there was a knock on the door. There stood two good friends: Rina Berto and Virginia Perkins, wives of the two chiefs at Point Adams. Just one look at their faces and LaVerne knew. She shook her head and kept saying no as if denying it could make things right again. Rina and Virginia walked in, and as gently as they could, they told her what had happened and of the loss of her husband. LaVerne just went numb as they sat her down on a chair. The women also said that her parents had been notified, and that they would be down in the morning.

LaVerne felt that it was odd, but for some reason, she was not thinking so much about the loss of her husband but that he would not be a part of their children's lives while growing up. The thought that they would never know their Dad was overwhelming. Virginia Perkins remained with Laverne the rest of the night as Rina departed to continue with her most unpleasant task.

Rina knew that Judy Hoban was at the Simonsen house and headed in that direction to finish the task she had been given. Arriving after 11:00 PM, she found Judy sitting in the living room talking with Colleen. Rina sat down next to Judy and began to tell her about the loss of the *Triumph* and possibly the crew including her husband, John. The Hobans had only been married for a short time and had great plans for a future with the Coast Guard and of starting a family. The information was very hard for Judy to comprehend, and it would take some time before she really realized that her husband was gone forever. Colleen told Rina that if Judy wanted, she could stay at the Simonsen house; or if she wanted, she could return home. In any case, Colleen would stay with her for the remainder of the night.

25

Empty Handed

Around 3:30 AM, Miller and his crew rounded the corner into the Hammond, Oregon, boat basin and tied up at the Coast Guard moorings. Not much was said between the crew as they mechanically did their duties of securing the *CG-36535* and making sure it was made ready to go out again if needed.

They found their vehicle at the moorings and drove it the half mile to the station. When they arrived, it seemed that every light in the station was on. The parking lot was full of cars that belonged to Coast Guard personnel and those of the local people. Entering the station, Miller found Chief Berto in the office and asked him if there was anything he could do. The chief told him there was nothing he could do now, and that he should go home to try to get some rest and return later on in the morning. Berto also told Miller to tell his crew to clean up and get some rest. After Miller had told this to Seaman Ponton and Engineer Dixon, he left the station and walked the short distance home. Joan met him at the door and put her arms around him, telling him that she was so happy that he and his crew were okay.

Miller headed directly to a chair in the living room and sat down. All he could say was "it should have been me" repeatedly. Joan tried to comfort him but felt that she did not really know how. Finally, he went to bed but was unable to really get any rest. He was referring to the fact that he had the duty that night and felt that he should have been the coxswain of the *Triumph*.

At the station, Seaman Ponton and Engineer Dixon took hot showers in an effort to warm up, and both changed into dry cloths. Ponton went into his room that he shared with three other men, two of whom were Seaman Sussex and Seaman Boatswains Mate Ralph Mace. He left the lights on and lay down on his bed, staring at the ceiling. He thought about his lost shipmates, and it was hard for him to imagine that never again would the three of them share stories about their lives, careers, and plans for the future.

Ponton lay there for a long time before he finally dozed off. Engineer Dixon was in the same situation as he had shared his room with Engineer Petrin. Both men would, in the next few days, assist in gathering all of the belongings of those lost to give to the wives and parents.

At 4:30 AM, BM1 Lopez entered the Hammond mooring basin and secured the *CG-36554*. An hour before, Webb had pulled the *CG-36554* into Cape Disappointment's boat dock and turned over the boat to Hernandez. BM1 Hernandez, on his return to Point Adams, reflected back on the night. He would be eternally grateful for the decision that was made earlier that night for him to take the *CG-36554* over to the cape and pick up Webb. He had never before, in his career, seen sea conditions so bad, and he knew that he was not someone who had the knowledge and experience to deal with it. From the time he had picked up Webb and they entered the bar area, the boat and crew were subject to some of the worst conditions they could imagine. They were constantly awash in breaking seas, and Hernandez had kept himself busy hanging on. He was the lookout for anyone in the water and was to let Webb know if any breaking seas were coming at them. After securing the *CG-36554* at the Hammond mooring basin, the crew returned to the station.

BM2 Ronald Brooks had gotten out of bed at 6:00 AM and checked on his wife and was out the door by 6:30 AM, walking toward the station. As he got within visual range of the station, he noticed an overabundance of vehicles in the parking lot. Outside the back door was a small group of men standing there, talking. Brooks recognized a couple of the locals, and he gave them a nod hello and thought it was a little strange that they did not say anything to him. As he opened the door and climbed the few stairs to the main deck area, a very ragged-looking Chief Berto met him.

Brooks asked the chief what was going on and was informed of the activities and events of the previous night. Brooks had a hard time believing what he was told. As with Miller, Brooks had the duty the night before and felt he should have been there. The chief explained to Brooks that he needed a well-rested boatswains mate to help him out in the office and possibly get underway with one of the lifeboats, and that was why he had not called Brooks back to the station earlier. This seemed to appease Brooks for the time being, and he busied himself by getting the remaining crew organized and reviewing everything that had happened the night before.

On the Washington side of the river at Cape Disappointment, it was a morning of turmoil and anguish over the loss of their shipmates from Point Adams and the near loss of the men from Cape Disappointment. The only thing Chief Porter could be thankful for was the safe return of all those involved in the search, and that six of his men found safety onboard the lightship. He would have gladly sacrificed his one remaining forty footer if it would bring back the men of the *Triumph* and the *Mermaid*. It was a most unpleasant day and would remain so for several days to come.

Chief Porter had contacted the pilot boat, *Peacock*, and asked them—if possible, when seas abated enough—to remove his men from the lightship. They said they would, but it took a couple of days before this could be done. In fact, the men could not be removed until the morning of 16 January 1961. The pilot boat brought the men across the bar where they were met by Chief Porter and his only remaining boat, the utility boat *CG-40421*. Chief Porter returned his crew to Cape Disappointment where they got ready to cross the river to Astoria, Oregon. The men were required to be in Astoria to testify before the board of investigation formed by the Coast Guard to collect and review the facts of the case.

BM1 John L. Culp

BM2 John Hoban

SNBM Ralph Mace

EN3 Joe Petrin

SN Gordon Sussex.

26

13 January 1961

In the morning hours of 13 January at Point Adams, BM1 Miller arrived back at the station. Once Brooks updated Miller on activities and directions he had received that morning, they both got busy putting together all the necessary reports and making the phone calls that needed to be done. Brooks had put together a list, which included informing the relatives of those single men who had perished the night before. Chief Berto was trying to get some rest and was lying on a bed that was in the designated sick bay next to the office. He had told Miller and Brooks to give him a wake up call if they ran into any difficult situations. They thought everything was difficult for them, but they knew the chief needed rest. About this time, Seaman Ponton walked into the office and asked if there was anything he could do. Miller asked how he was doing, and Ponton stated that he was okay other than numerous abrasions and pain to most of his body but nothing that would cause him not to perform any duties that might come up.

Brooks mentioned the fact that he had overheard Ponton saying, at one time, he had taken a class in typing. Ponton said that he had, but he was not that good at it. That was enough for Miller and Brooks, and they immediately assigned him to the station office to help with the mountains of paperwork generated by the incident. Although the loss of five of his shipmates was very painful for BM1 Miller and his wife, Joan, the loss of Engineer Petrin was even more so. Miller had become friends with Petrin. He had taken an immediate liking to Petrin, and Miller and his wife had invited him to their home for dinner many times. Miller kept remembering the last time he saw of Petrin; he was on the bow of the *Mermaid*, fighting for his and the crew of the *Mermaid*'s lives. For the rest of Miller's life, he would never forget that moment and how helpless he felt when he could do no more than operate the lifeboat to the best of his ability.

Before 8:00 AM in the morning, Miller's parents arrived and were elated to find that their son had come through everything okay. Later in the day, the parents of Joe Petrin arrived at the Coast Guard station and then were invited over to the Miller household. LaVerne Culp's parents had also arrived and gave the much-needed comfort to her. They would assist her for the next several days in making funeral arrangements for her husband, John.

From 6:00 AM to 9:45 AM, BM1 Webb and Engineman Meyer from the light station at North Head had driven down to the beach just north of the north jetty. They had not been asked to but felt driven to continue the search for their shipmates. Their efforts proved fruitless, and they reluctantly returned to the station.

Later in the afternoon, the remains of the *Mermaid* would wash ashore right off the Long Beach approach. A large truck with a winch was sent from the Coast Guard station Cape Disappointment to the scene and winched the boat up to the dry-beach area. There was not much left of the boat, and after a quick inspection, it was determined that no victims were still aboard. A large crowd had gathered including many local fisherman who marveled at the Bergmans' ability to maneuver their boat for such a long period of time and to remain out of harms way as long as they did. It was almost inconceivable for the Bergmans to do this for several hours by putting the boat in gear forward and reverse and using engine power to do so. To do this spoke a lot for the Bergmans' and the boat's ability to survive as long as they had before they were finally overwhelmed by the breaking seas. Beach patrols by the Coast Guard and the local residents were conducted through 18 January 1961 but without any further sightings of wreckage or victims.

Then, on 19 January, a body identified as that of Bert Bergman came ashore near the beach approach of Oysterville, Washington, which is twenty miles north of the Columbia River entrance. At least Bert's family had some final closure for him as his brother and the rest of the coastguardsmen would never be found. There was a lot of animosity among the local people on the Washington side toward the Coast Guard over the loss of the Bergmans and their boat. It was felt that there were many mistakes made by the Coast Guard from the start of the case until the Bergmans were lost.

Many of the local fishermen were tuned in to their marine-and-citizen-band radios that night, listening to what was going on, and had many questions that they felt needed to be answered. One of these questions was why, after the forty footer took the *Mermaid* in tow, did they not go to sea to avoid the rougher shallows of the bar area. Instead, the decision was made to tow her toward buoy 1, which would put everyone in more danger. Why, once the boats arrived at buoy 1 to await the arrival of the *Triumph*, did Murray allow both boats to drift farther into the vicinity of buoy 7 where it was even more hazardous? The Coast Guard would never answer some of their questions, and hard feelings would be held for many years.

The Coast Guard Cutter *Yocona* had remained outside the river most of the night and into the next afternoon. The Coast Guard Cutter *Modoc* had arrived near the lightship at 8:30 AM, and the *Yocona* instructed them to lay off, awaiting further instructions. The *Modoc* had steamed all night in very rough seas to render any assistance they could. It was a relief for them to lie to and relax some even though, at the lightship, the winds were gusting to sixty-three miles per hour with seas to fifteen feet.

At 3:00 PM on 13 January 1961, the *Yocona*, as was the *Modoc*, were released from the active search and directed to return to their respective homeports. At 5:45 PM, the *Yocona* tied up starboard side to pier 3, port dock in Astoria, Oregon. The *Yocona* crew that missed the ship because of its quick departure met her when she arrived. When they boarded the ship, they all set about securing the many things that had come adrift the night before. It was not long before everything was shipshape, and the *Yocona* was ready to go again if called upon. Respite was not so easy for the *Modoc* as she and her crew had to steam late into the night to arrive home at Coos Bay, Oregon.

27

The Board of Investigation

The official Coast Guard Board of Investigation would convene in Astoria, Oregon, on 14 January 1961 and continued through 16 January. Over this time period, all those involved in the case would give testimony regarding their involvement. Among those attending were members of the Columbia River Bar Pilots Association and Mr. Roy Gunnari, owner of the fishing boat *Jana-Jo*, who had originally called in to report that the *Mermaid* needed assistance. Also present were the Coast Guard station personnel and boat crews, and to represent the families of the Bergman brothers were two local fishermen from Chinook, Washington: Mr. Allan Malchow and Mr. Lawrence Prest.

It was not until 1:00 PM on January 16 that the crew from Cape Disappointment were able to be removed from the lightship. They would arrive at the board of investigation later that same afternoon.

The investigative report reads almost verbatim as to the daily logs of the stations, units, and others involved. It states more about what happened than about trying to find out why it happened. Why it happened as it did would focus more on blame, which the Coast Guard seemed to want to avoid. A problem cannot be fixed if it is not recognized whether it be mechanical, design flaw, or a personnel matter.

In an interview with BM1 John Webb from North Head Light Station, at the time of the incident, he said when called on the stand to testify, he was sworn in and answered many questions. Webb had previously been assigned to station Point Adams for six years and was a qualified coxswain for the *Triumph*. While testifying, he volunteered some information about the *Triumph* that he thought might be relevant to the case. He stated that while he was at Point Adams, an engine swap had been done on the *Triumph* the year before. He also stated that upon completion of the installation, there remained an opening between the engine compartment and the forward

berthing area. This seemed to be something the investigators did not want
to hear, and they dismissed him.

The investigative report also states that the proceedings were conducted
with open doors except that witnesses from the same unit were excluded while
others from that unit were testifying. This seems to contradict a statement
from the engineer of the *CG-40564* from station Cape Disappointment.
Engineer Lowe stated that when they arrived at the hearing late in the
afternoon of 16-January, everyone was seated in the room together. Everyone
did listen to the questions and answers from those sworn in. Did that have an
influence on how the others testified? As Lowe said in a 2007 interview, the
answer in his case was yes. He did not elaborate but said there were things
he wanted to say but held back volunteering anything. While preparing for
this book, the author interviewed Lowe extensively over a two-year period.
He offered a wealth of firsthand information concerning 12 January 1961.
He always stated that he just wanted the truth to come out. It was felt by
this author that Lowe continued to hold back things that were bothering
him about that day that nearly cost him and his shipmates their lives.

In the investigation, no one ever brought up the question of why neither
station, Point Adams or Cape Disappointment, conducted a running plot
on a marine chart of all boats out on the call. If this had been done, a
pattern could have been seen on exactly where these boats were positioned
along with a time written on the chart. Doing so would only be as accurate
as the positions given by the boats. Tides, currents, time, and weather are
also factors that could be placed on a marine chart and would show that a
more hazardous situation was materializing. This is called dead reckoning
navigation and would use the information as stated above. With the
Mermaid in tow, it would have showed that *CG-40564* could have been
steadily going toward the more hazardous areas of the bar. Then seeing
this situation, someone at one of the stations could have raised the alarm
and warned Murray so he could try to get farther offshore.

Onboard Coast Guard ships, while they are underway, it is required that
they keep an active plot while at sea every hour. While in confined waters,
the time is reduced to every fifteen minutes so that the ship's position can
be more actively monitored to warn in plenty of time of any dangers. This
is not the case with small boats operating in heavy seas. It seems that this
should be done from a shore station with the information relayed to the
boat. This would seem to be the more prudent thing to do as it would lead
the boat crew to the safe operation of their boat.

During the January 1961investigation, it was consistently stated that the *Triumph* was a self-righting lifeboat. The following is a report generated by the loss of the *Triumph* on 12 January 1961. The report is an investigation on facts concerning the righting abilities of the MLB *Triumph* and ordered by the commander of the Thirteenth District and dated 28 February 1961.

The findings of fact, opinions, and recommendations of the board as set forth in the attached report of investigation, forwarded, and marked approved.

> Conclusion 43 (i) appears to be based upon some misconception as to the design of the 52-foot wood motor lifeboats. The designed range of stability for these vessels is 140, degrees. Once capsized, they will generate no self-righting moment arm on roll of less then 40 degrees. It would thus be easily possible for the CG-52301 (Triumph) to have remained capsized for a substantial period, even if there had been no substantial flooding of the forward compartments. Whether, there was such flooding forward, as was surmised by the Board of Investigation will never be known.

What the above report means is that if all watertight integrity is maintained and the boat was rolled to or past 140 degrees, she would most likely remain there for a time until a wave would move the boat to at least an inverted 40-degree roll.

The report continues as follows:

> An inclining experiment (ability to self-right) was performed on the CG-52300 (Invincible), in 1956, after a new engine had been installed. This experiment disclosed only small changes in the stability characteristics of the vessel. Range of stability was reduced from 140 degrees to a 137 degrees, met centric height from 1.97 to 1.84, and maximum righting arm from 1.45 to 1.25.

This means that on rolls in excess of 137 degrees, the boat might not recover for a time unless some wave action came along. And the report continues as follows:

> Since there has been no significant weight or design changes in the vessel since this last experiment, no further inclining

experiment is contemplated at this time. However, an evaluation board has recently completed a comprehensive survey of the CG-52300 (Invincible at Coos Bay) and reported upon its condition. Some minor defects of watertight integrity were disclosed and are being corrected. In addition, some minor design changes have been recommended. These will be the subject of separate correspondence. End of finding of fact."

It can be assumed from the original plans that the two wood fifty-two footers built in 1935 and 1936 also showed the findings of the action of convening authority, namely, the board of investigation. Why these statistics were ignored from the start by allowing those who operated the boats to assume that these boats were self-righting is unbelievable. Even after the stability tests were conducted on the *CG-52300* (*Invincible*) in 1956 and found that they were not self-righting as everyone was led to believe, no operating restrictions were placed on these boats. Up to 12 January 1961, everyone that should have been aware of the boat's abilities always stated that these boats were self-righting.

The men from Cape D. that were out the night of 12 January 1961. Left to right, BM1 Darrel Murray, SN Acie Maxwell, EN2 Terry Lowe, SN Jim Croker, SNBM Larry Edwards.

28

The Men of Point Adams: Where Are They Now?

Boatswains Mate Senior Warren C. Berto

BMCS Berto and his wife, Rina, remained in the Coast Guard until he retired in 1974 as a chief warrant officer. Between 1961 and 1974, Chief Berto went on to command the buoy tender *White Holly* in Ketchikan, Alaska, and on another tour as commanding officer of the buoy tender *Blue Bell* based out of Portland, Oregon. His final assignment was as officer in charge of the aids-to-navigation station, Kennewick, Washington. Berto and his wife, Rina, retired to Dayton, Washington, where they bought and operated a bowling alley for many years. His wife, Rina, passed away several years ago; and he has since sold his business. Berto is fully retired and still lives in Dayton.

Boatswains Mate First Class Willis Paul Miller

BM1 Miller and family served a few years in the Thirteenth Coast Guard District including eighteen months at Coast Guard Light Station Clallam Bay and then to Cape Disappointment as the executive officer under Chief Tom McAdams. While at the cape, he was promoted to chief and was transferred to governor's Island, Alameda, California. Here he served as a company commander to new recruits. From Alameda, Miller transferred in 1968 to the 378-foot Coast Guard Cutter *Boutwell* based out of Boston, Massachusetts. The family resided in the area until Miller was promoted to chief warrant officer W-2, and he received a set of orders to the buoy tender *Laurel* based out of Morehead City, North Carolina. Between 1971 and 1977, Miller served onboard the *Relief* lightship out of Seattle,

Washington, as executive officer to the group commander, Group Coos Bay at Coos Bay, Oregon, executive officer to the group commander, Westport, Washington. Miller's final assignment was in 1977, as the commanding officer of the buoy tender, Coast Guard Cutter *White Lupine* based out of Rockland, Maine. After a short time on the *Lupine*, Miller became ill, and the doctors diagnosed him with pancreatic cancer. On August, Miller transferred back to his home in Seattle, Washington.

The Coast Guard promoted Miller to CWO-4 on 1 September 1977. He retired on 100 percent disability on 5 October 1977. Miller passed away on 4 November 1977 at age forty-two, and just a few days before, he would have been in the Coast Guard for twenty-three years.

From the time of the *Triumph-Mermaid* tragedy, Miller was bothered by the fact that if he had been aboard the *Triumph*, maybe there would have been a different outcome. This was the same thoughts as many of the survivors had from that night. What was of a major concern for Miller was that he kept seeing Joe Petrin on the bow of the *Mermaid* just before the *Mermaid* was lost in the turmoil of a large breaking sea. His wife, Joan, continually supported him and asked him many times if he thought that maybe he needed some counseling. Miller told her he wanted to continue with his career in the Coast Guard, and that if he did ask for counseling, it would come to the attention of higher-ups, and he might be blocked from further advancement.

Boatswains Mate First Class John L. Culp and Wife LaVerne

On 19 January 1961, John was laid to rest with full military honors at a cemetery just outside of Warrenton, Oregon. Many of John's shipmates and friends of the family attended the funeral. The Gold Lifesaving Medal was later presented to John's widow, LaVerne, by the Thirteenth District commander, Rear Admiral P. V. Colmar. In 1979, the Coast Guard dedicated a new building at the Training Center, Alameda, California, in memory of BM1 John L. Culp.

Soon after the funeral, LaVerne moved the family to Port Angeles, Washington, and moved in with her parents. From 1961 to 1972, LaVerne divided her time between raising her children and working at various jobs in the area. In 1972 and until she retired in 1998, LaVerne worked in various positions with the local school district. Her daughter, Cheryl, stated that her mother did not date anyone for almost fourteen years until she met a local man, Art Dixon. The couple was married in July 1974 and still resides to this day in Port Angeles.

LaVerne made sure of one thing over the years, and that was for her children, John and Cheryl, to have a proper upbringing. They are both grown with families of their own and doing fine.

Engineer Third Class Gordon Huggins

Huggins was the only survivor from the *Triumph*. He endured what no man should have to do, being trapped inside the *Triumph* after she had capsized. He considers himself a very lucky man as do the other survivors from that terrible night. Gordon was not offered any psychological help after what happened to him and would not obtain any until 1995. He remained at Point Adams for almost another year, performing the duties of a boat engineer. Incredibly, while on a case aboard a forty footer from Point Adams, Huggins was again washed overboard only to be retrieved quickly. He was not wearing a lifejacket as the weather and seas, at the time, did not seem to require the need for one.

In 1962, it was time for Gordon to put in for a transfer, and he applied for an eighty-three-foot patrol boat outside of Seattle. Instead, and unbelievably, he received a set of orders to Eldrid Rock lighthouse in Alaska. This duty was extremely isolated, and no place to send a man that had, not so long ago, gone through what Gordon had endured.

Huggins spent what he felt was an uneventful year at the lighthouse. He would wake up in the night with the cold sweats not realizing that the ordeal he had gone through and tried to put behind him was the cause of his discomfort. After Huggins left Alaska and his enlistment was up in 1966, he moved back to Vancouver, Washington. Here, he applied for a job as a Clark County deputy sheriff and was accepted. He was a patrol deputy and retired in 1993 with over twenty years of service.

All the time Huggins was a deputy, he had recurring dreams about 12 January 1961 that haunt him to this day, but he finally found some help. Every year, Navy and Coast Guard ships come up the Columbia River to attend the Portland Oregon Rose Festival. The ships would stop at Astoria, Oregon, and take on civilian and military passengers that would ride the ship the one hundred miles to Portland. Gordon managed to get aboard one of the Coast Guard ships and made his way to the bridge to observe the passage. While leaning against a rail and looking out a window, he happened to strike up a conversation with a civilian man standing next to him.

Gordon mentioned that he used to be in the Coast Guard and volunteered what had happened to him aboard the *Triumph*. The man asked him if he had gotten any kind of help. Gordon told him no as he had thought that he was dealing with it himself but, for the last several years, was having continuing problems with nightmares. The man identified himself as a civilian employee at the Veterans Hospital in Portland, Oregon, and gave him his card and told him to contact him as soon as he could, and he would get him in for some counseling. The help would include a complete evaluation with an assessment of the kind of care they could give him. As soon as Gordon got home, he contacted the hospital, and they made an appointment for him. Huggins said the treatment he received was very helpful, and that he should have had it right after 12 January 1961.

Gordon and his wife, Patricia, are completely retired now; and they reside on the banks of the Cowlitz River in Castle Rock, Washington.

Seaman Douglas Ponton

Ponton was a crewmember aboard the *CG-36535* with BM1 Miller as coxswain. All of the men from both stations had a cross to bear, and for Doug, it was double. First, he had to live with the fact that if it were not for him taking the watch for Seaman Sussex so Sussex could go aboard the *Triumph*, he would have been there, and Sussex would have been safe. Secondly, when they found the *Mermaid* out there in those terrible seas and saw his shipmate, Petrin, catching the line he threw, seeing the terror on Petrin's face was an image that would stay vivid in Ponton's mind for years.

In 1991, there was a thirty-year reunion at the Astoria Maritime Museum for all those involved. Over one hundred people attended the reunion. Ponton wrote in a notarized statement that it was sad, but Mother Nature just beat them down. This is true, but there were many other factors, as stated in this book, for the tragic outcome of that night.

When Ponton had mentioned that he had some typing training, he was recruited to help fill out the many reports. He did not know then that this type of work would be his career choice with the U.S. Coast Guard. After Ponton's service at Point Adams, Ponton went on with duties within the Coast Guard and retiring, after many years, as a master chief yeoman. Ponton now resides in Nevada.

Engineer Third Class Larry C. Fredrickson

Fredrickson was the engineer onboard the *CG-36535* with BM1 Miller, and Fredrickson attended the thirty-year reunion in Astoria. Since then, he has been difficult to locate. For a reunion of Point Adams, Cape Disappointment, and the Motor Lifeboat School Memorial Day weekend 2007, extensive research had been gone into, trying to locate him, without results. The last heard of, Fredrickson was living in the Cottage Grove, Oregon, area. It is imagined that since 12 January 1961, Larry has gone through similar thoughts as the other men.

Boatswain Mate First Class John C. Webb

Webb was the coxswain of the *CG-36554*. Webb would receive the Coast Guard Commendation Medal along with many others that were out the night of 12 January 1961. Soon after the tragedy, Webb went on to receive a gold star in lieu of a second Commendation Medal for climbing down a 140-foot cliff and rescuing a man from drowning in the surf near Long Beach, Washington. It would always seem that John would be where needed, as a year later he was transferred to the Coast Guard Station, Quillayute River at La Push, Washington. This coastal area is most unforgiving with very few beach areas that are clear of rocks and reefs.

Webb would receive the Gold Lifesaving Medal for his actions in saving the lives of those aboard a yacht that had grounded on a reef twenty miles north of La Push. The yacht was destroyed, and heavy damage was done to the thirty-six-foot lifeboat Webb was operating. In spite of this, they all made it to safety north to Neah Bay, Washington.

Webb would remain in the Coast Guard, retiring after twenty years as a master chief boatswains mate. After retirement, John and his wife, Vallory, moved to the Warrenton, Oregon, area where he operated a charter boat and office and soon would get into the commercial crabbing business. The Webbs purchased a very suitable crab boat and operated the business for many years.

The Webbs are now completely retired and reside in their home near Astoria, Oregon.

Engineer Second Class Larry E. Dixon

Dixon was the engineer aboard the *CG-36554*. As with all the others that were out on the boats on 12 January 1961, Dixon has his memories of the tragedy. He remained at Point Adams for most of the remainder of 1961. He also remained in the Coast Guard with over twenty years of service, retiring in 1974 as a senior chief engineer. After retirement, he and his wife moved to Independence, Oregon, where he worked at several different lumber mills in the area. Dixon finally retired from the mills in 1999 after twenty-four years.

Boatswains Mate First Class Hernando Lopez

Lopez transported the *CG-36554* over to Cape Disappointment to pick up BM1 Webb. Very little is known about Lopez after he left Point Adams. It can be surmised that he, most likely, would have gone back to the bigger Coast Guard cutters. This would not be hard to understand after what all of them went through on 12 January 1961. It has been said that Lopez could not stop talking about his experience that night, and it really bothered him.

Fireman Apprentice Ronnie E. Jansson

Jansson was an engineer who would act as a seaman onboard the *CG-36554*. Jansson is another person that has been hard to locate. He did remain in the Coast Guard and finished his enlistment; but nothing, after this, is known about him.

Engineer Third Class Junior Meyer

Meyer was one of the men that found Huggins alive on the beach. Meyer, at the time, had just arrived at his new duty assignment at North Head Lighthouse. He had, prior to January 1960, been assigned to Point Adams station; this is why he is mentioned here along with the men from Point Adams. Meyer remained in the Coast Guard and retired after more than twenty years as a master chief machinery technician. After the Coast Guard, he worked for many years using the skills he learned and applied them in the heavy equipment and gas turbine power generation industry. In 2005, Meyer completely retired. Meyer and his family reside in the Reno, Nevada area.

John Jr. and Cheryl Culp in front of the Memorial set up at the entrance to station Pt. Adams 1962-63.

John Jr. and Cheryl Culp in front of the Black Lake Memorial, Ilwaco, Washington, 2007.

CG-40514 close in to beach south of the South Jetty summer 1961. BM1 Miller at the controls. Port side aft is Gordon Huggins shortly after being washed overboard.

29

The Men of Cape Disappointment: Where Are They Now?

Boatswains Mate Chief Doyle "Stan" Porter

Porter remained at Cape Disappointment through 1962. During this time, he took a crew from Cape Disappointment to San Francisco and took delivery of the *CG-52314*, the new fifty-two-foot steel motor lifeboat. They transported her to the Columbia River and to her new home at the Coast Guard Station Cape Disappointment where, to this day, she performs in some of the roughest waters in the world. Chief Porter went on to earn a commission as an officer in the Coast Guard and retired as a lieutenant commander in 1976. He had finished his career as the group commander at Coos Bay Station, Coos Bay, Oregon. Stan and his wife, Peggy, moved to Florida where they bought a home and a four-acre orange grove. Stan also kept his hands in the marine field, owning a small tugboat and a business called Triumph towing. He and Peggy make annual trips to the West Coast to visit their many friends they came to know while in the Coast Guard.

Boatswains Mate First Class Darrell Murray

Murray was the coxswain of the *CG-40564*, which was lost the night of 12 January 1961. He remained at Cape Disappointment until January 1962. Darrell would remain with the Coast Guard until 1977 when he retired as a senior chief boatswains mate. There is not a day that goes by that Darrell does not think about 12 January, and how fortunate that he is to be alive today. It was by the grace of God that the thirty-six-foot motor lifeboat happened onto him and his crew that were hanging onto the bottom of the capsized *CG-40564*.

Darrell had thought that he came through everything without any injury with the exception of a sore back he had shaken off soon after the tragedy. This back problem would surface some years later, and it was a constant battle between Murray and the Veterans Hospital before he got the injury recognized and treated after so many years had gone by as a prior injury that was done in the line of duty. After retirement, Darrell held many different jobs, but he is now completely retired. He and his wife, Kathryn, reside in Billings, Montana.

Engineman Second Class Terry Lowe

Lowe was the engineer onboard the *CG-40564* that was lost. Terry was trapped inside the cabin of the forty-footer. He managed to get out and join the other two crew members on the bottom of the capsized forty-footer. He just about lost his life again while trying to get aboard the lightship from the *CG-36454*.

Lowe remained in the Coast Guard and retired a master chief engineer in 1979 with over twenty-one years of service. He and his wife, Patricia, moved to Newport, Oregon, where Terry worked another twenty-one years at the Georgia Pacific Mill in Toledo, Oregon, retiring for good in 2003.

For over forty years, Terry has suffered from terrifying nightmares about the incident on 12 January 1961. Lowe was another one to suffer without any help, for his problems, from the Coast Guard. It is surprising how well in life most of the men have done while suffering posttraumatic stress from their ordeal. Terry seems to be doing rather well and says that the only time now that the nightmares come back is when he gets a visit from some of his old shipmates, and they start to talk about what happened. He says he can deal with his memories better now than before and knows that it is also his shipmate's way of venting what has been inside each of them for so many years.

Seaman Boatswains Mate Larry Edwards

Edward's was a member of the Coast Guard Reserve out of Yakima, Washington, serving his two-year active duty tour at Cape Disappointment. Edward's was the coxswain of the motor lifeboat *CG-36454*. No amount of training could have prepared someone for what Edward's and his crew would go through on 12 January 1961. It was in part his skill at operating the thirty-six-foot motor lifeboat and just plain luck at being at the right place at the right time. If it were not for this seemingly lucky happenstance, there would have been a far greater loss of life.

For his efforts, Edwards was at first recommended for the Silver Lifesaving Award, which was later amended to the Gold Medal Award. Edwards remained at Cape Disappointment for the remainder of his tour and then returned to his home town of Yakima. Being the recipient of the Gold Lifesaving Medal offered many enhancements; one of which was the awarding of points toward advancement. Edwards wanted to take advantage of this and enlisted in active duty and went on to retire after twenty years as a chief boatswains mate. There is not much known about Larry's post—Coast Guard activities, but he does reside somewhere in the coastal area of the state of Oregon.

Seaman Acie Maxwell

Maxwell was the crewmember onboard the *CG-40564*; and it was, as with the others, an experience he would never forget. When the forty-footer flipped over, he was thrown clear. Somehow, he managed to get on top of the capsized boat where, if it were not from his efforts in helping Engineer Lowe and Boatswains Mate Murray, they might not have survived. Maxwell remained in the Coast Guard for a few years working in the cook rating. He got out of the Coast Guard and since has worked and resided in the Port Townsend, Washington area.

Seaman Apprentice James Croker

Croker was aboard the motor lifeboat *CG-36454* and, to this day, still like the others, has vivid memories of 12 January 1961. Croker, in 1961, was transferred to the Coast Guard Cutter *Storis* in Kodiak, Alaska, where he finished his four-year enlistment. Croker returned to his hometown area of Portland, Oregon, where he worked for ten years in the auto body field and then started work as an ironworker. He retired from this trade after thirty-three years. Croker and his wife, Donna, have been married for forty-two years.

Fireman Brian H. Johnson

Johnson was the engineer aboard the *CG-36454*. Johnson served the remainder of his tour at Cape Disappointment and then returned to his native Astoria, Oregon. Johnson worked for sixteen years as a Columbia River bar pilot, guiding shippers into and out of the river entrance. In 1985, Johnson, along with his brother, established Johnson Oil Co. at Astoria, Oregon. About this same time, he was elected to the Board of Directors of Central Oregon Community College in Prineville, Oregon. Johnson passed away in 1988 at the young age of forty-nine.

Engineer Second Class Grover G. Dillard

Dillard was attached to Cape Disappointment and resided in government housing at North Head Light Station. He along with Meyer located and rescued Huggins at Benson Beach. It is not known if Dillard made a career in the Coast Guard. His whereabouts are unknown.

30

The Boats and Aircraft Involved

The motor lifeboat *Triumph* and the utility boat *CG-40564* were lost with barely a trace of anything other than life jackets and rafts showing up on the beach. It was rumored that a life ring from the *Triumph* washed ashore in San Francisco Bay. This has not been substantiated.

The lifeboat *CG-36454*, after rescuing the three men from the capsized *CG-40564* and making it to the lightship, was documented as breaking its mooring line to the lightship and sinking in the area. In a telephone interview in 2007 with BM1 Murray with this author, he stated that shortly after the 12 January incident, the boat washed up on the beach somewhere on the northern Oregon coast. He stated that the boat was salvaged and is now in Hawaii somewhere. In a telephone interview with EN2 Lowe in 2007, he stated that BM1 Murray talked to him about some mysterious cover up by the Coast Guard about the loss of the *CG-36454*. This boat did the job it had been built to do on 12 January 1961 by safely getting the six men to the lightship before sinking. There is no valid reason for the Coast Guard to want to cover up anything about this boat. The boat was written off by the Coast Guard as surveyed and lost in the line of duty. I have asked the persons that stated they salvaged this boat for some kind of documentation, such as a newspaper article, and have received nothing.

The lifeboat *CG-36554* went on to serve many more years at station Point Adams until the station closed in 1967 and then at Cape Disappointment for several more years. These boats could have served at other stations along the coast as needed. The *CG-36554* is now a shore-side memorial exhibited at the Coast Guard Station, Westport, Washington.

The lifeboat *CG-36535*, like the *CG-36554*, went on to serve at Point Adams and Cape Disappointment. This boat had the distinction of being the longest serving thirty-six-foot lifeboat in the Coast Guard. During her final years of service, she did duty with the Coast Guard's Hole-in-the-Wall gang at Depoe Bay, Oregon. The nickname Hole-in-the-Wall gang came about because of the location of Depoe Bay, Oregon, and the Coast Guard station there. The access to the bay is through a very narrow entrance in the rocky cliffs on the Oregon coast hence the nickname. It was sometime in the 1980s that the *CG-36535* was finally retired and put on the excess property list. Supposedly, a maritime museum on the East Coast had acquired her; and for many years, the boat has been reported to be stored in a warehouse.

The Coast Guard Cutter *Yocona* and *Modoc* went on to serve many years at their respective bases in Astoria and Coos Bay, Oregon. The *Yocona*, toward the end of her career, served several years based out of Kodiak, Alaska. Both ships were retired from service, placed in the mothball fleet and eventually surveyed by the government and either sold or scrapped.

The Columbia River lightship was retired after her duties were taken over by giant sea buoys. Since her retirement, she has been acquired by the Astoria, Oregon Maritime Museum. The ship was placed in a floating exhibit at the museum. This ship can be boarded for a tour daily, year round.

The pilot boat *Peacock* was retired many years ago and replaced by a steel self-righting-type boat that had been constructed in Germany. The replacement served for many years and was replaced by others that were also built to serve in the harsh environment of the Pacific Northwest. The *Peacock* of 1961 was sold and served in Alaskan waters in the fishing industry. It is rumored to have been lost several years ago. As of 2008, the Columbia River Bar Pilots have initiated the use of helicopters to take off and put aboard pilots to suitably equipped ships. This is a much safer procedure than the use of boats for this purpose.

Only one aircraft is traceable, and that is the *UF-1240*. This aircraft served the Coast Guard into the late sixties. It was recorded lost in the Gulf of Mexico with all hands during a search-and-rescue mission. The cause of the plane going down has not been determined. Neither the plane nor her crew has been found. Even though these aircraft served faithfully for many years with the Coast Guard, there were several that were lost for unknown reasons or premature flare ignitions inside or from engine failure during critical takeoffs.

The Albatross aircraft served with the Coast Guard, Navy, and Air Force for many years. Their primary missions for the military were of the search-and-rescue nature. There are a few flying to this day, owned by civilians, and most have been converted to the turbo-prop-engine configuration.

The new steel MLB Triumph CG-52314 1960's She was delivered to Cape Disappointment in 1962.

The CG-52314 outbound, Cape D. lighthouse and lookout tower in background.

The Pilot Boat Peacock that replaced the 1961 Peacock. This boat served the Columbia Bar Pilots into the 1990's and was much more suitable.

31

The Motor Lifeboat School

The following is a fitting statement to add at this time and represents the one major training criteria initiated for Coast Guard boat crews that operated the lifeboats on the coasts of the United States. It was written by Chief Warrant Officer Giles M. Vanderhoof, U.S. Coast Guard, and was written in March of 1993. It reads as follows.

Statement of events leading up to the establishment of the Thirteenth District Motor Lifeboat School (later in 1980 the National Motor Lifeboat School) by Chief Warrant Officer Giles M. Vanderhoof, U.S. Coast Guard Retired.

After the introduction of the forty-four-foot motor lifeboats into the Coast Guard fleet in 1962, it became quite evident that the quality of training for heavy-weather coxswains was falling below acceptable standards. This was caused in part by the ability of the forty-four-foot motor lifeboat to survive even though the skills of the operators were steadily declining. I witnessed lack of training and skill while being stationed on the East Coast during the mid sixties and found it even more prevalent upon returning to duty on the West Coast in the Thirteenth District in 1968. I requested an audience with then Thirteenth District chief of staff, Captain Richman, and chief of operations, Captain Emerson. During this meeting, I discussed my feelings about the lack of suitable training of boat coxswains, which was resulting in loss of civilian life and property along both coasts of the United States. Both Captain Richman and Captain Emerson agreed, sighting numerous cases here in the Thirteenth District. I was asked what my solution to this problem would be. I proposed a two- to three-week saturation-training course to be established preferably at the Coast Guard Station Cape Disappointment, Ilwaco, Washington.

They both concurred with my recommendation if I was willing to set up the school and make it work. I agreed, and limited funds were made available for a small school building. I was assigned TAD (temporary attached duty) to Cape Disappointment. I was to oversee the school's construction, decide on what the training should consist of, write the curriculum, pick instructors, and obtain enough equipment and supplies to place the school in operation.

It was decided that the need for cross-training boatswains mates and engineers existed, so a three-week BM/Coxswain-Engineer and a two-week Engineer/Coxswain course was set up. This cross-training would allow either to take over the duties of the other in the event that one became incapacitated.

The original teaching staff consisted of me, Boatswain Mate Master Chief Jack Wood, Boatswain Mate First Class Larry Hicks, and Engineer First Class Cummings. A boat maintenance crew of three seaman, three fireman, plus a third-class yeoman to assist with all the paperwork was assigned. The original goal was for a minimum of 50 percent underway training. Our average was close to 65 percent. I personally participated in all underway training.

Three forty-four-foot motor lifeboats were assigned TAD from various Thirteenth District units and the use of Cape Disappointment's forty-two footer and forty-four footers when available. The first class was convened in January of 1969. Subsequent classes were run through April, alternating between the boatswains mate and engineer courses. The engineer classes were later discontinued because they were slowly, but surely, turning into the Thirteenth District's engine-training and troubleshooting school, which was not the original intent.

In May of 1969, I turned the motor lifeboat school over to Master Chief Jack Wood, my leading instructor, and returned to my permanent duty assignment. I was presented the Coast Guard Achievement Medal for my efforts in this endeavor.

Looking back to those years Mr. Vanderhoof talks of, it seems that his accomplishment in taking the helm and having the fortitude deserves a lot more than the Coast Guard Achievement Medal as recognition. It was through his efforts that the school was started and continues into 2008. The school has adapted its training over the years to include new technologies and the operation of the Coast Guard's newest lifeboat, the forty-seven footer.

It has become a national school and has included in its classes over the years many coxswains from foreign countries such as Canada and England. Since the beginning, there have been many commanding officers and officers in charge of the school along with the best instructors the Coast Guard could muster.

Many of the instructors have been picked from the ranks of those that had been prior students of the school. Being the commanding officer or instructor at the school is considered a coveted position, and all of those chosen feel honored to serve. In the early seventies and shortly after Mr. Vanderhoof's tour of duty, a new officer in charge was chosen—Master Chief Tom McAdams. He put to use a phrase his grandmother would recite whenever a child or grandchild said, "I can't." This slogan remains today over the docks used by the National Motor Lifeboat School and the men and women of Cape Disappointment and says, "Can't Never Did a Dam Thing But Try Always Did."

It is considered that many lives and much property has been saved through the training offered by the school over the years. This has been accomplished by the constantly updated equipment of the Coast Guard and the curriculum offered at the school. There have not been many losses of lives and boats in a single instance within the Coast Guard since the 12 January 1961 incident. This does not mean that it could not happen again. Men and women of the Coast Guard are not only taught to become surfman, but are much better equipped to deal with any situation and make the right decisions in times of peril.

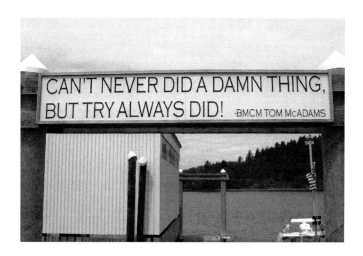

Statement originated from Master Chief Tom McAdams. To this day you can see this statement across the docks at Cape Disappointment. "Can't Never Did A Damn Thing But Try Always Did"

32

What is New?

As said earlier, many improvements were coming into place at the time of the tragedy on 12 January 1961 and would continue to this day. In 1962 and 1963, the use of the first primitive wet suits was introduced to the boat crews of the Coast Guard. By primitive, it meant that they were very basic. They were made of quarter-inch black rubber glued together into a two-piece suit that covered the legs, arms, and torso. Booties and a head cap were made of the same material. To get into these suits, talcum powder had to be sprinkled inside. In a few years, the suits were made with a nylon lining for easier access. Then came what was called the farmer john suits. International orange in color, they had many zippers along the legs, arms, and torso. When unzipped, a man could step right into them with his clothes on.

Both of the aforementioned survival suits were wet suits that allowed water to enter and then would be warmed by the body heat of the person wearing the suit. Both of these suits would provide a great deal of protection for a time, if they were worn properly, and the person had to enter the water.

Present day survival suits worn by Coast Guard boat crews are dry suits. A long underwear is worn against the skin with a fleece covering over it that is referred to as a bunny suit. The dry suit is worn over the bunny suit. Once properly worn, no water is allowed to enter and reduces body heat loss for the wearer. All of these suits are made of very durable material and are in international orange color. Over the dry suit, each person wears a type 3 life vest, which—unlike the old kapok life jackets—gives the wearer freedom of movement. A pyrotechnics vest is worn over the life vest. The pyrotechnics vest has a survival knife, signaling mirror, mouth-operated whistle, and day-and-night hand flares attached to it. Also included are several hand-launched red-in-color pencil flares and a small strobe light that, when activated can be seen for many miles. Each person wears a helmet similar to a football helmet. Attached to this helmet is a manual or water-activated Epirb (emergency positioning identification rescue beacon), which when activated sends a signal via satellite to search-and-rescue stations on the ground, giving an exact location of the person wearing the device. Each Epirb will have a code entered into it identifying the wearer that will also be sent with the distress signal.

In 1962, the first of the remarkable forty-four-foot motor lifeboats would enter the service. By remarkable, it meant that they were a breakthrough in new construction back then. They were the first lifeboat produced to replace the thirty-six-foot lifeboats. These boats were self-righting with a hull made of welded steel that was twenty times as strong as regular steel and an aluminum superstructure.

They had twin diesel engines that gave them a cruising speed of twelve knots. These boats, as were the new fifty-two-foot lifeboats, were not without problems from the start. Every time something came up, solutions were quickly found, and the problem corrected. When operating in heavy sea conditions, all crew members were required to wear a harness that had short lanyards attached that could be hooked to multiple eyebolts situated at convenient locations around the boats. It was also in the early sixties that full helmets similar to football helmets were required wear in heavy weather operations, and this practice continues to this day in 2008.

There were over one hundred of the forty-four footers constructed by the U.S. Coast Guard, and they were in continuous use from the early sixties until the 1980s. The forty-seven-foot motor lifeboat replaced them. Almost all of the forty-four footers are still in use today at various duties in other countries, and some have been sold to nonprofit organizations such as the Sea Scouts and on the civilian market. During the many years of operation by the crews of the Coast Guard, there are only two recorded losses; one of which was the loss of a forty-four footer out of Quillayute River at La Push, Washington. This boat was lost on the rocks of James Island with multiple loss of life. The other was a forty-four footer out of Juneau, Alaska, when somehow she was put hard aground on a reef in the area. Both boats were a total loss. What could be recovered was surveyed and scrapped.

If you happen to find yourself taking a trip to the Astoria, Oregon area, be sure to put on your list a visit to the Astoria Maritime Museum. Here you will find many fine exhibits from the maritime traditions of the Pacific Northwest.

The very first forty-four-foot motor lifeboat that was constructed and used for many years on the Oregon and Washington coasts, the *CG-44300*, is shown here inside of the very large front windows of the museum in a beautiful tribute to the U.S. Coast Guard and the men and women who operated the boat.

With the construction of the final two steel fifty-two footers, it would place the four of them at strategic Coast Guard stations at Coos Bay and Newport, Oregon, and Westport, Washington, and Cape Disappointment at the mouth of the Columbia River.

Over the many years, the fifty-two footers have performed rescues on the coasts and as far offshore as 150 miles, assisting disabled fishing boats. They have accomplished this from calm winds and seas to hurricane-force winds and thirty-foot plus sea conditions. At times, there was damage from the elements to these boats and injuries to their crews, but there has been no reportable loss of any crewmember lives while onboard. If you were to visit any of the stations where these boats are based, you would find that they have been maintained to a condition as they were when new. There has been talk around the Coast Guard that maybe these four boats should be retired. When asked how they would be replaced, the Coast Guard cannot say that they have a boat that could meet the standards that the fifty-two footers have for ruggedness and survivability.

As of the year 2008, it has been learned that the lifespan of the fifty-two footers for Coast Guard use would be expanded for another ten years. This would put the age of all four boats to over sixty years. The price to maintain these boats for that time seems to be small compared to what they have accomplished over the years. As good as these boats have been maintained, it can be imagined that they will not last forever, and they will eventually succumb to metal fatigue of the steel hulls or aluminum cabins.

The Columbia River Lightship and the Giant Sea Buoy that replaced her. The buoy has been replaced by a much smaller one. The Buoy and Lightship are on permanent in water display at the Astoria Maritime Museum, Astoria, Oregon.

Cape Disappointment boathouse, docks and station in the 1970's. Everything including staff is much larger with the addition of the National Motor Lifeboat School.

The CG-44336 was attached to Cape Disappointment throughout her service in the Coast Guard. These boats replaced the 36 foot MLB's and in turn were replaced by the 47 foot MLB's starting in the 1980's.

The 47 foot MLB's are now along with the four 52 foot MLB's the only lifeboats in service with the Coast Guard. The 47 footer was built for multi-service in that they were built for heavy weather use are self-righting along with a huge increase in speed over prior lifeboats at 25 plus knots. As far as electronics are concerned everything is 1st class and updated as needed. In this configuration the 47 footers also fit right in with the Coast Guards Home Land Security duties.

Epilogue

With the passing of CWO4 Willis Paul Miller in 1977(coxswain of the *CG-36535*), his wife, Joan, asked a longtime shipmate of his to write and deliver the eulogy. This person was Master Chief Boatswains Mate Thomas D. McAdams.

Eulogy

Paul Miller, The Rarest Of Men

I met you, Paul Miller, in the morning, when the fog was rising from the bay.
You reported in for duty and a friendship was born that day.
A young man in your twenties, the Coast Guard was your career.
And you served it with devotion, and of the ocean you had no fear.
And now you are back on the Columbia, Where the lifeboat, Triumph, went down.
On a stormy night, with waves of fright, and her five man crew would be drowned.
But you took a crew and went out that night.
And searched in those breakers until it was light.
With unwavering devotion until the last.
You distinguished yourself in an impossible task.
Time and again with lifeboat and crew, you met the challenge and knew what to do.
Your course was set, and noon would pass.
The flight of years, as you accomplished your tasks.
And evening approached, and you advanced with the years.
An inspiration to men, which was distinctly yours.
From Seaman recruit to Chief Boatswain Mate.

You advanced up the ladder and made every rate.
And thousands of calls for assistance at sea.
Have been born by you so diligently.
Then on to Warrant Officer you navigated with ease.
As you set your course over life's changing seas.
Now the morning I met you has long passed.
The noons and evenings swept by so fast.
But I'll always remember your fidelity.
Your respect for virtue, and love of wife and family.
Now darkness has come. But in vain we call.
Your virtues are on the tablets of love and memory of all.
Now you've advanced up the last ladder, to the realms on high.
And our friendship, like brothers, will live till I die.

On 11 January 1991, the survivors and families of the 12 January 1961 tragedy got together at the Astoria Maritime Museum for a thirty-year reunion. The commanding officer at Cape Disappointment at the time was a guest speaker for this event. He stated that what happened on 12 January 1961, tragic as it was, would never happen again with the modern equipment used today and with the well-trained boat crews of the day. Later that very day, the fishing vessel *Sea King*, which was in a sinking condition, was being towed by the *Triumph II* (*CG-52314*). The *Sea King* was lost in the same general area where the 12 January 1961 tragedy occurred. There was loss of life—both Coast Guardsmen and civilians that were aboard the *Sea King*.

It just goes without saying, "Never say never."

About the Author

Gary J. Hudson was born and raised in Spokane, Washington and, at the age of eighteen, signed up with the U.S. Coast Guard. Before this time, he had never heard of the Coast Guard. Actually he was in downtown Spokane looking for the Air Force recruiting office when he saw a sidewalk billboard showing a picture of a Coast Guard boat speeding through the water. A sailor was on the bow with a life ring in his hand. Hudson thought to himself this was the exciting life that appealed to him. After walking into the recruiter's office, he found that in a very short time, he was signed up for four years and was off to recruit training for three months at Alameda, California.

Those three months did not appeal to him at all and neither did his first experience at sea aboard an icebreaker, the U.S. Coast Guard Cutter *Northwind*. The *Northwind* was heading for the Antarctic in 1958. Along with many others, Hudson found himself huddled on the flight deck near the warm exhaust fan vent from the engine room. Everyone was very seasick. This misery lasted for two days until the seas and the rolling action that only an icebreaker could have abated. To the men on the flight deck, it was as if a miracle had happened. To Hudson, it was not exactly what he had envisioned outside the recruiter's office.

After one and a half years aboard the *Northwind*, Hudson was transferred as a seaman to Willapa Bay Lifeboat Station, which was located twenty miles north of the Columbia River. For the next eighteen years, he served at several stations on the Washington and Oregon coasts. Notable of these was the Point Adams Lifeboat Station at Hammond, Oregon, where he served as a seaman in 1960. He was transferred to a light station on 1 January 1961. Again he was at Point Adams in 1964-65 as a boatswains mate third and second class and also had two tours of duty across the river at Cape Disappointment in 1968 and 1969 and 1974 and 1975 as a first-class boatswains mate and chief boatswain mate respectively.

All of his duties at lifeboat stations involved operating all of the unit's lifeboats and utility boats. He was qualified as a heavy-weather coxswain aboard the thirty-six-foot, forty-four-foot, and fifty-two-foot motor lifeboats. Hudson participated in many rescues off the coasts of Washington and Oregon and served with many of the best Coast Guardsmen of the period. Among many awards and citations he had earned during his career, one of the most notable was the Coast Guard Commendation Medal for his actions on a case off the mouth of the Columbia River.

Other than the at-sea tour onboard the *Northwind*, he served aboard the Coast Guard Cutter *Cape Romain* out of Ketchikan, Alaska, as a first-class boatswains mate and as a chief boatswains mate aboard the cutter *Confidence* out of Kodiak, Alaska. His final duty was as officer in charge of the small icebreaking tug, the cutter *Chock* out of Portsmouth, Virginia. Hudson retired from the Coast Guard in 1979 and followed up with operating charter boats out of Ilwaco, Washington, jet boats from Laughlin, Nevada, to Lake Havasu and a trip as a deckhand aboard a tugboat to Prudhoe Bay, Alaska.

Hudson capped off his going-to-sea experiences with serving for fourteen years as the boatswain aboard the Army Corps of Engineers Hopper Dredge *Yaquina* based out of Portland, Oregon. The *Yaquina's* operations carried her and the crew from southern California to Alaska. He retired for good in 1999. He and his wife, Joyce, reside in a home they built on the banks of the Cowlitz River at Toledo, Washington.

REFERENCES

U.S. Coast Guard assistance reports for Point Adams and Cape Disappointment for 12 January 1961.

Ships logs and weather reports for the U.S. Coast Guard Cutter Yocona and the Columbia River Lightship from the National Archives covering a period from 9 January to 16 January 1961.

Tide and current predictions at the mouth of the Columbia River for the month of January 1961 from NOAA (National Ocean Service, Silver Spring, Maryland).

U.S. Coast Guard Board of Investigation, dated 14 February 1961.

Doug Ponton notarized statement, 6 March 1991.

Darrell Murray transcript interview, 7 April 2000.

University of Oregon news archives for the Coos Bay World, December 1960.

The numerous handwritten reports and hundreds of e-mails from those that were there or had firsthand knowledge of the incident.

INDEX

Edwards Brothers, Inc.
Thorofare, NJ USA
October 25, 2011